The Unfinished Teacher

The Unfinished Teacher

Becoming the Next Version of Yourself

Michael Lubelfeld, Nick Polyak,
and PJ Caposey

ROWMAN & LITTLEFIELD
Lanham • Boulder • New York • London

Published by Rowman & Littlefield
An imprint of The Rowman & Littlefield Publishing Group, Inc.
4501 Forbes Boulevard, Suite 200, Lanham, Maryland 20706
www.rowman.com

86-90 Paul Street, London EC2A 4NE

Copyright © 2024 by Michael Lubelfeld, Nick Polyak, PJ Caposey

All rights reserved. No part of this book may be reproduced in any form or by any electronic or mechanical means, including information storage and retrieval systems, without written permission from the publisher, except by a reviewer who may quote passages in a review.

British Library Cataloguing in Publication Information Available

Library of Congress Cataloging-in-Publication Data Available

ISBN 978-1-4758-7315-3 (cloth)
ISBN 978-1-4758-7316-0 (pbk)
ISBN 978-1-4758-7317-7 (ebook)

Contents

Acknowledgements	vii
Foreword *Kim Radostits, 2022 Illinois Teacher of the Year*	ix
Preface	xv
Introduction	1

SECTION 1: PERSONAL GROWTH: WHO YOU ARE AS AN INDIVIDUAL

1	Being a Great Teammate	7
2	Awareness	15
3	Personal and Social-Emotional Health	23
4	Financial Health and Wellness	33

Teacher Essay 1: Being Self-Aware or "With Great Power Comes Great Responsibility" *Jon Bogie, Fourth-Grade Teacher*	43

SECTION 2: INDIVIDUAL AND INTERPERSONAL PROFESSIONAL GROWTH AND CHANGE: WHO YOU ARE AS A TEACHER IN THE CLASSROOM AND WHO YOU ARE AS A PROFESSIONAL

5	Curriculum, Standards, Assessment, and Data	49
6	Meeting the Needs of Each Child	57
7	Technology	65
8	Teacher and Staff Morale	75

Teacher Essay 2: My Unfinished Journey 81
Eric McFadden, High School Teacher

9	Conclusion	87
	References	91
	About the Authors	95

Acknowledgments

All

We all want to thank the reviewers and endorsers of our book, the professional collegiality is meaningful, and we are so grateful to you for your time, energy, wisdom, and support!

Mike

I want to thank the teachers with whom I work and from whom I learn each and every day. I want to thank the teachers with whom I taught side by side for so many years. I want to thank the Board of Education in North Shore School District 112 for their belief in the value of our teachers as well as in supporting our "inspire, innovate, engage" motto each day.

I want to acknowledge and offer heartfelt thanks to Andrea Trudeau, a no-shush librarian in the Deerfield Public Schools, for friendship, collaboration, and for critical and frank review of the manuscript and for her feedback in this process. I want to acknowledge and thank Jon Bogie, fourth grade teacher at Wayne Thomas School in Highland Park, Illinois, for taking the time to write an essay for the book. I want to acknowledge and thank Paul Solarz, author of *Learn Like a Pirate: Empower Your Students to Collaborate, Lead, and Succeed* for his honest, thoughtful comments and feedback!

I want to dedicate this book to my wife Stephanie, my daughter Maya (a teacher in training), and to my son Justin. They are my teachers every day!

PJ

I would like to thank two of my all-time favorite teachers I have had the pleasure of working with for contributing to this book. Aaron Sitze, your work as a critical friend was invaluable to us reformatting and reimagining large sections of this book. Kim Radostits, you are the best. Your foreword is inspirational and motivating, exactly like you are in the classroom. We are better for your efforts.

Personally, this book was written at one of the most demanding times of my career. Thank you to my family for the unconditional love, unending support, and the precious time needed to continue to pursue my professional ambitions and desire to leave my own little ding on the educational universe.

Nick

I want to acknowledge and thank the teachers, support staff, administrators, and the Board of Education at Leyden Community High School District 212. I am blessed to go to school every day with some of the finest educators in the world. Together we "Educate, Enrich, and Empower" the students in our communities, always with a focus on "What's Best for the Kids." I am a better educator and a better person for having the opportunity to serve as their superintendent.

And I dedicate this book to my amazing wife, Kate, and our four children, Chase, John, Ben, and Gabe. I'm sure, to them, Dad is always either working or involved in some crazy project—this book being the most recent. I appreciate all of them and the constant support and encouragement they give me every day.

Foreword

A little over a year ago, I was making my way down to our school gymnasium when I saw our State Superintendent walking into my school followed by a parade of balloons and cameras. "Dr. Ayala, what are you doing here?" I blurted out confused, only to be ushered up to my room where over a dozen of my students and I learned that I was being named the 2022 Illinois Teacher of the Year.

The fanfare and interviews that followed are now a blur, likely because of the flood of emotions that came with being awarded an accolade attached to what I would consider to be one of the most noble professions in the world. I had dedicated the last fifteen years of my life to my students, my colleagues, and my practice and I was excited to share what we had accomplished on a much greater scale.

Another part of me, however, was full of anxiety and unanswered questions about what a sabbatical away from the world I had grown to love would be like and how I could continue to make an impact from outside my building. That was until I remembered something that PJ Caposey said to me my third year of teaching—"change is only scary when you perceive it as a loss."

That advice came because of some schedule changes I had proposed that were ill-received by my peers. The proposal was one I thought would be best for kids, but involved changes which would have impacted my colleagues in several ways I hadn't considered. It was my first mistake as a teacher leader (though I didn't see myself as one at the time), and my initial reaction as an already self-proclaimed wallflower was to cower in my classroom and never propose another change again.

Instead, a few weeks later, PJ checked in on me and approached me with the idea of pursuing a master's degree in educational leadership. While he was describing it, I could not have imagined a crazier idea. When I got home and talked to my family about it, however, the conversation evolved from worrying about what I would do with a degree in leadership into how I would be impacted by the journey.

Little did I know that this program and that line about change would alter the trajectory of my career and my life. In the years that followed, after looking critically at sample classrooms for my coursework and doing research on best practice, so many of the systems and routines within my own classroom evolved. I found myself in a constant state of reflection, research, and revision as I continued to observe the students in my classes, our interactions, and our outcomes.

I did a much better job of documenting the things that were working so I could replicate them and dream up ways to improve. Before I knew it, I started to find inspiration for improvements all around me.

Additionally, I bounced back from that initial leadership mistake from my third year of teaching and worked with my colleagues to take steps in overhauling a small after-school homework hub for freshmen. No longer could I contain, within the four walls of my classroom, my desire to do better for students and to be better. Week after week, we came together and discussed the students in that after school program until we eventually turned it into a multitiered system of support for *all* freshmen.

Together we found ways to improve the relationships we were building not only with our students, but with their families and with each other. As a result, we created a system that was so refined that we were able to decrease the number of course failures in our freshmen class from 237 in 2007–2008 to only 14 in 2019, the year before the pandemic. That progress couldn't have happened if it wasn't for a team that was willing to be flexible and embrace change as a constant process.

Then, several years later, after examining the ways a sense of belonging and a sense of pride made a difference for our students, one of those team members and I started talking about how a similar cohort model could benefit new hires. As a result of a big wave of retirements and some nonrenewals, we knew we were going to have over a dozen new staff members that year.

We did have a mentorship program ready to launch, but those who had been through it agreed that it lacked consistency and school connectedness. Thanks to an administration that allows us to take risks, we were given permission to scrap the old model and designed a new cohort that features local professional development provided by experts within our district.

These experts provide real-world examples from our school community and utilize the tools and technology we have readily available, offering new hires the ability to try what they are learning in real time in a collaborative setting. This new model reaffirmed yet again that change can bring value if you're brave enough to reimagine your systems and programs and stay unfinished. As a result, we saw a group of new teachers not only willing to stay, but willing to grow and willing to lead.

This growth mindset regarding change has also served me to overcome other big obstacles in life. In fact, for twenty-nine years I lived in a small-town community made up of three short blocks and around sixty homes. In the almost three decades of my time there I could describe what every corner and crevice of that community looked like, without fail, because it never once changed.

Certain homes had the same gardens tilled year after year, others stood in need of new roofs and siding to no avail. It was though it was a postcard stuck in time with no vision or desire to stray from the norm. And then, in April 2015 everything changed as an EF4 tornado ripped through our town and destroyed almost a third of the homes in its path.

What was left of my side of town could best be described as the set of a horror film, and the community I had grown to love with all its imperfections became a shell of itself. This change was scary . . . it seemed like nothing but a loss.

But, in the seventeen months that followed, after thousands of hours were invested by volunteers, contractors, and community members, we saw a community rebuilt stronger than ever. The homes erected stand on the same plots of land, but the interiors and exteriors now show off new colors and angles. The landscape has been reimagined with more gardens than ever before. There are new street lanterns, a beautifully renovated park now full of smiling children and driveways that have been widened and paved to invite more guests to enjoy our lovely little town.

What I find even more inspiring than the quick rebuild of these structures, however, was the way I saw the people in our community being rebuilt. The storm destroyed our homes, but it is evident in so many ways that it did not destroy our spirit. Within forty-eight hours, when families were given permission to start to clean up, you began to see so many of us looking past the loss and looking toward what could be.

I remember repeating that line about change not being scary to anyone that would listen. It became a mantra I would follow in some of the most frustrating of times. Together, we became a community looking toward hope and made a rebuild come to fruition one step at a time.

Those seventeen months included meetings, paperwork, and infrastructure work that needed to occur for a rebuild to happen. It was a long, daunting process that we all had to work through while also maintaining full-time jobs and some semblance of a life. In addition to simply being a survivor, I was appointed to the long-term recovery committee to provide community member voice to all leadership decisions.

I was able to utilize that degree I never thought I would use in a capacity I never could have imagined. I leaned into those skills of collaboration and communication that had served me so well in my school community and I hoped it would lend itself to building stronger connections with my neighbors. As time progressed, relationships among community members became stronger as we all leaned on each during different parts of our rebuild.

Eight years later, and you'll still see neighbors checking on one another on every sunny day and now sharing meals on holidays. Even more surprising to me is that not a day goes by where you don't see at least one community member making a change to their newly rebuilt home. Unlike the community that stayed steadfast in its appearance in the past, this newly reborn community is one that has and will continue to be "unfinished" in the most beautiful of ways.

As a teacher, I watched this phenomenon happen all over again in March 2020. At the onset of the pandemic, as schools shut down, you saw teachers and students ripped away from their safe space, their routines, and the relationships that had been built. And yet, humanity triumphed again as teachers, administrators, students, and community members from around the globe started coaching and supporting one another.

Once again, I witnessed schools and communities pull together resources for families in need and demonstrate creativity to provide students with a sense of belonging and pride through socially distanced parades and social media campaigns.

In terms of academics, when we got the call that school was shut down, I was in the process of National Board renewal. I was one section away from a completed entry that was about delivering a meaningful unit of instruction and no longer had in-person access to my students.

After several days of panic, I tapped into that advice from early on in my career yet again and chose to use the circumstances as an opportunity to grow and discover new ways to connect with students. I reframed my lessons as "Radventures," where my students and I worked alongside each other to figure out what would work best for all of us during that period of our lives, and I asked them for honest feedback.

A few weeks in, I concluded that the solutions we had curated together were worth sharing out. I was elated to see that when I offered professional development workshops over Zoom to my district on how to run synchronous and asynchronous lessons over a platform I had just learned, it was *full* of educators across grade levels and content areas willing to collaborate to do what was best for our students.

Once we got over that fear of loss and started to reimagine what teaching could look like, we were unstoppable. When I speak to crowds of veteran educators now, as Illinois Teacher of the Year, I often say that if we were to compare ourselves to the versions of us that were in our classrooms in February 2020 we would see that so many of the issues in education have stayed the same, but we have grown as educators, we are stronger, and we have proven time and again that we are capable of amazing things.

If we continue to use our newly expanded tool kits and to work together with the network we grew during the pandemic there is no doubt we will see great things happen in the future of education. We need to move past the loss we felt and look toward the hope. I know firsthand that this can be done, because I have seen the monumental changes humanity is capable of when we work together.

Though I do not wish these last two scenarios on others, I believe that both gave me a gift of perspective. Both scenarios forced me to change in an abrupt way. And yet, in education, we do not need an abrupt change. We are given a reset button every single summer. Every year, we can pause, recharge, reflect, and reinvent pieces of ourselves, our curriculums, and our routines.

We, as educators, are given the choice and the gift to stay unfinished. When I reflect on the surprise I had when I saw my State Superintendent in my building, I recognize that the shock came from never once seeing myself as the best teacher in Illinois. In fact, most days I can't even see myself as the best teacher in my hallway.

What I can say is that I am working tirelessly to give my students the best experience possible and that is something I have been able to do by allowing myself the opportunity to take risks in the classroom and to evolve. Just like my newly rebuilt town that now refuses to settle for "good enough," I take pride in my surroundings, my work, and my people.

During this sabbatical, I have been inspired by so many educators who share a similar mindset across my state and the nation. In fact, since February, I have been given the opportunity to interact with fifty-four other phenomenal state teachers of the year. Each of us is honored to have accepted a rare accolade that most do not get to experience in the profession. And yet, when we get together, our conversations aren't about what we've accomplished in the past.

Our time together has organically become centered around collaboration, innovation, and hope for the future. Every moment that we have spent walking around the Smithsonian Institution, Google, or the White House, or just from workshop to workshop, features someone saying "wouldn't it be awesome if . . ."

We are perpetual dreamers with a desire to make the system better for all that are in it and for those who join it in the future. We believe that we belong to each other in this profession and that we collectively have the power to change the world, one student at a time. We won't cower from change, we seek it. We are like so many of you and want to be better for students. And, to do that, we must stay connected, curious, and unfinished.

Kimberly Radostits, NBCT
2022 Illinois Teacher of the Year
2023 National Teacher Finalist
Oregon Jr/Sr. High School
krad@ocusd.net

Preface

IT'S TIME WE HAD A TALK

The past twelve months may well have been the hardest of your professional career. The irony is that this was written with the intent of being consumed in 2024. The reality is that whether someone reads this in 2024 or 2034, it will likely be true. Each year of your professional life may be the hardest of your career.

There is a good chance. However, it was also the easiest twelve months you will have for the rest of your working life. Whenever you are reading this book may also be the toughest of times or the smoothest of times. Regardless, our charge to you is to stay unfinished and to commit to becoming the next version of yourself!

Recently (as we write this book) we have been reflecting on the impact of the worldwide global pandemic, ideally the only one for any of us in our lifetimes! Yes, last year (2022). Yes, the year with the *mask controversy*. *Yes, the year with the learning loss*. Yes, the year when someone above you created a new initiative that you only half-heartedly agreed with. Yes, the year when the "tough" class came through your classroom or building.

That year. That year was the easiest year of the rest of your career. Since we're unfinished, we can handle this and move forward to become the next versions of ourselves!

Think that is impossible. Look around.

Ask your friends and colleagues. Find someone with twenty years of experience and ask them if the teacher's job has gotten any easier. Inquire if they think the demands, pressures, and sequence of changes are any easier today than they were in 1990, 2000, 2010, or 2020.

The answer is no. The answer is always no. The answer is no in our industry and in every other industry. We are constantly racing against time and progress—and they are not slowing down. Even though the COVID-19 years will go down in history as unusually challenging, the challenge is real and always present.

If you want to avoid this being the case, there are limited options:

1. Expect less of yourself. If you lower your personal expectations and find a personal status quo, your professional life *may* get easier.
2. Expect more of yourself. In the famous words of Jim Rohn, "Don't wish for fewer problems; wish for more skills." Get better. Grow. The only way the job gets easier is if your personal progress outpaces the progress of the problems you will be charged with solving.

Read that again. It may be the most important sentence in this book. *The only way the job gets easier is if your personal growth outpaces the progress of the problems you will be charged with solving.* You can either embrace mediocrity or embrace change.

IT IS THE ONLY OPTION

So, as we see it, we have two options—get on board with being unfinished or risk being completely miserable. If we attempt to do the same things for kids in 2033 as we do today, we will be woefully ineffective. Very rarely is someone who is ineffective at their job fulfilled by their job and happy in their professional life. We wrote this book to help you embrace the concept of being unfinished and to help you become the next version of yourself with positivity, professionalism, and purpose.

Teachers create the conditions for all professions (it's an old adage, but we believe it's timeless and true). Looking forward to the future of society, it's essential that we educators create conditions in support of teachers. Believing in the concept or mindset of unfinished is one step on this massive journey. The journey is existential, and it is ever present.

Teachers are unfinished in part because our work is not yet complete. When we are called to teach, we are called to influence the world. When we are called to shape the future, it's incumbent upon us to imagine what we want in the world. As the proverb says, one generation plants the trees and another gets the shade.

The beauty of our work is that we can forever change the future of a child's life and therefore our society in general. The difficulty is that as we plant the seeds (to extend the analogy), we often never know which ones will grow and flourish. We are constantly sowing seeds, but not only do we not get to enjoy the shade, but we often never know which trees even fully blossom and bloom.

The ability to embrace the unknown and unquantifiable impact of our work is what makes truly extraordinary educators stand out from the rest. As an example, Vander Ark and Liebtag (2021), share the twenty-five most important issues in the world as adopted by world leaders in the United Nations Sustainable Development Goals (designed to provide a road map to a better future). The first five are:

1. No poverty: End poverty in all its forms everywhere.
2. Zero hunger: End hunger, achieve food security and improved nutrition and promote sustainable agriculture.
3. Good health and well-being: Ensure healthy lives and promote well-being for all at all ages.
4. Quality education: Ensure inclusive and equitable quality education and promote lifelong learning opportunities for all.
5. Gender Equality: Achieve gender equality and empower all women and girls. (32–33)

Our profession is present in all five of these goals! The unfinished teacher is on a mission, a calling, a passion, a journey that really has no end. The journey is to make the world a better place. The world can be "the world" or it can be your classroom at Anytown School. And pardon the cliché, but we do this one child at a time, one classroom at a time, and one school at a time.

OKAY, 2033 MIGHT SEEM FAR AWAY. BUT IT'S NOT.

The change in our world is constant. Our kids are different than they were ten years ago and will be vastly different ten years from now. Our communities are changing. Our world is fundamentally different and will continue to evolve. In education, we must adjust to them and our world (more importantly, their world), or we will become dangerously irrelevant.

Thankfully, too, the world is unfinished, and ideally it too is striving to become the best version of itself. What do we do if the organization in which we work is keeping us behind or even oppressed in some way? The unfinished teacher either works within that system or seeks a better system to serve. It's a harsh reality. Administrators are starting to realize they need to create better conditions for teachers and in collaboration with one another they can create better, more relevant systems.

So, as educators, we have one major and powerful choice. That one option is to stay relevant. That one option is to compete. That one option is to serve our kids with integrity. And perhaps most importantly, that one option is to be personally happy. Collectively, that one option is to stay unfinished.

Embrace change. Love the grind. Have a deep, hard, introspective conversation with yourself that it will never be easier to be great at your job. And be okay with that realization. Work on becoming the next version of yourself, constantly iterating and reiterating. Don't try to become the best version of yourself, there is no such thing.

And it is our hope—deep in our souls—that accepting the fact that it will never be easier energizes us all. You were not put on this earth to be average. None of us were. You have chosen to be a part of the best profession in the world. We can change lives every single day. It is an awesome responsibility, but an even more incredible opportunity.

Stay unfinished. Become the next version of yourself.

Introduction

The Unfinished Teacher: Becoming the Next Version of Yourself is a book for, about and dedicated to teachers. Educators are the most important professionals in our society, and arguably in any society. They are the ones who create the conditions for all other professions.

We wrote this book because, in our more than seventy-five years of combined educational service as teachers and administrators at the school and district levels, we are profoundly proud of teachers and educational support staff members in our service. We are committed to the mindset of unfinished learners, leaders, and teachers.

The mindset of being unfinished gives us the grace, road map, and playbook to keep trying and to keep succeeding as if our lives depended on it. We hope the road map for teachers to thrive and remain unfinished as they continually improve their outcomes are found in the two sections, eight chapters, and two teacher vignettes of this book! Each vignette is after the last chapter in a section.

In our 2021 book *The Unfinished Leader: A School Leadership Framework for Growth and Development*, we identify six frames or lenses leaders should lead through to become the next version of themselves (empathy, equity, adapt, develop, communicate, unfinished). In this book, we focus on teachers becoming the next versions of themselves.

We're focusing on teacher impact within the concepts of personal growth, and professional growth. Our aim is continuous growth, development, reflection, and improvement so we can all sustain the education profession.

While the primary audience of this book is the classroom teacher, we believe anyone invested in the growth and support of the greatest profession in the world, education, would benefit from reading the book. Our nation is at a time of peak politicization of the profession and experiencing a dramatic teacher shortage.

This book is our small contribution to trying to not only recruit new teachers to the profession, but to honor the work of current educators and serve to re-recruit them to the profession. Simply, our nation needs you. Our kids need you.

The book is organized into eight chapters in two sections. In every chapter we close with a summary, forward thinking points related to the chapter called Tomorrow Takeaways, and Reflection Questions for further study, review, analysis, and action.

In section 1, "Personal Growth: Who You Are as an Individual" we focus on four main subject areas in chapters 1 through 4: being a great teammate, awareness, personal and social-emotional health, and financial wellness. Below we share each chapter with the content sections listed.

Chapter 1: Being a Great Teammate
Teamwork, Autonomy, Self-Awareness, Collaboration, Coaching, Changes in Personnel

Chapter 2: Awareness
Our Lived Experiences, The Path to Self-Awareness, Reflection, Professional Learning, Your Students, Blind Spots, Awareness Promotes Empathy

Chapter 3: Personal and Social-Emotional Health
Call to Action, Teaching Is a Demanding Job, Causes of Burnout, Physical Health, SEEDS—Simple Ways to Stay Healthy, Gratitude, Reclaiming Your Why

Chapter 4: Financial Health and Wellness
Reminders, Money 101, Begin with the End in Mind, Financial Stress, Supplemental Retirement, Investments, Invest in Yourself, Financial Literacy

There are teacher vignettes after section 1 and section 2. We feature one from a fourth-grade teacher, and one from a high school business education teacher. The path to any type of personal and professional growth begins with a firm understanding of who one is and where they are on their personal journey. The four chapters in section 1 help the reader understand multiple ways they can work to better understand themselves and their individual blind spots, tendencies, and superpowers. By discovering who we really are, the freedom to become who we desire to be is unlocked.

We cannot serve others when we are struggling ourselves. Whether the origin of that struggle is physical, mental, or social-emotional, we have a responsibility to ourselves and those we serve to continue to invest in ourselves as much as we invest in those around us. We'll outline strategies that can be used to move ourselves from the brink of burnout back to reclaiming our why and thriving in the profession.

In the spirit of staying unfinished, we must *never* stop investing in ourselves and our own health. By taking care of ourselves we create the pathway to better take care of others. Far too many educators do not think about their financial health and well-being until they approach retirement. In the chapter on financial wellness, we outline simple strategies that can be used to help ease stress related to finances in general.

In section 2, "Individual and Interpersonal Professional Growth and Change: Who You Are as a Teacher in the Classroom and Who You Are as a Professional," we address these main concepts in chapters 5 through 8: curriculum, standards, assessment and data, meeting the needs of each child via an equity lens, technology, and morale and culture. Below we share each chapter with the content sections listed.

Chapter 5: Curriculum, Standards, Assessment, and Data
The Art and Science of Teaching, Curriculum, Standards, Assessment

Chapter 6: Meeting the Needs of Each Child
Voices, Equity, Collective Efficacy, Treating Each Child as They Need to Be Treated, Response to Intervention (RtI) / Multitiered System of Supports (MTSS)

Chapter 7: Technology
Technology as an Enabler, Leverage for Good–Embrace the Reality of the Student World, Gamify/Artificial Intelligence (AI)/Augmented Reality (AR)/Mixed Reality (MR), Seeking Professional Development and Growth, Student Lens/Agency, Technology Is Ubiquitous, ChatGPT and Generative Artificial Intelligence

Chapter 8: Teacher and Staff Morale
It Is All of Us, Impacts on Morale, Dimensions of Culture, Hearing the Teacher's Voice, Partnering in This Work

The Unfinished Teacher becomes a master of the curriculum and leverages the most effective teaching methods possible to create optimal learning conditions. School districts range from standardized curricula to individualized curricula. Teachers work within the rules and expectations of their schools. Yet, they are always focused on improving and making the most of the resources available daily for each child.

Being unfinished in this domain reflects an understanding that state tests will change, benchmarks will shift, and modalities will become more complex; our challenge is how to use this change to get better, to improve, to stay current with what is to be taught, how it is to be taught, and how it is to be assessed.

The authors acknowledge that there may be an existential disconnection between the teacher's desire to stay relevant and the fact that the world is changing faster than we are. So, teachers must adapt. And there is also the construct that "The teacher works within the rules and expectations of her school." So, what if the rules and expectations of the school (district, state) are not keeping up? What are the options for the teacher? Adapt and *don't* follow the rules? Or follow the rules and *don't* adapt?

This is a dilemma for us all, and the ideal scenario would be for mutual, collaborative professional problem-solving to help an organization avoid that dilemma. Equity has become a huge buzzword lately, and at its core, it simply means meeting the needs of each child every day. If scaffolding is needed, then scaffold. If reteaching is needed, then reteach. If technology is needed, then use technology. The critical teacher piece with equity is knowing how to know what you need to know.

This means being a questioner: Where are my students? How much support do they need at home and at school? What am I, as a teacher doing to meet their needs best? Do I have the support I need to provide equitable instruction?

The Unfinished Teacher is an equity ninja; they create conditions of welcome, rigor, positivity, and justice for each child under their care. The unfinished teacher is also a policy ninja. They understand the rules, regulations, expectations, and community norms, and they look for ways to impact and improve all of them. They do what is best for the child as they navigate the politics in the classroom and in the community.

This book embraces the concept of technology as an enabler for augmenting and enhancing education, teaching, and learning. In addition to the enablers, the concept of being unfinished calls for the teacher to learn and apply how to use tech enablers to best amplify student voice and, ultimately, student learning. Opening one's mind to the possibility of technology and the tools related to it vs shutting it down will best serve the teacher in their journey.

We also reflect on morale and our collective duty toward morale in our school systems. Evolving into a teacher leader and a school leader, not at the expense of one's mental and physical health, but integrated into the next version of the professional you are becoming. There is always a pull at the metaphorical rubber band that represents us. We want to stretch ourselves to keep the band fresh and alive, but we need to avoid too much stretch that breaks us. Thank you for taking the time to invest in yourself to demonstrate that you are an unfinished teacher focused on becoming the next version of yourself!

Section 1

PERSONAL GROWTH
Who You Are as an Individual

1

✣

Being a Great Teammate

"Build a team so strong that they don't know who the leader is."

—Unknown

Guiding Question: When we can accomplish so much more together than alone, why is it so challenging, at times, to truly form a team?

A Teacher Said to Us: "Am I supposed to feel like I'm competing against the other teachers in my building? With assessments and evaluations, it feels that way. I prefer to see my colleagues as teammates where we can make each other better."

TEAMWORK

There was a healthy debate in a graduate course one of us taught about whether we would prefer to have someone who is a great teacher and a horrible staff member or someone who is a great staff member and an average teacher. The reason for the intensity of the debate is that it was so relatable.

There are far too many educators who may be amazing in their classroom but either do not know how to be a member of a successful team or simply are not interested. The point of this chapter is to reinforce that to be an amazing educator, you must not only be great in the classroom, but also an incredible teammate for your colleagues. It's about collective efficacy.

One of our first mentors told one of us that teaching is the second-most-private thing you will ever do. You can let your mind wander for what number one would be. We share this advice because it was absolutely the *worst* advice any of us have ever received in education.

None of us work in isolation. Correction, none of us must work in isolation and the very best among us choose not to.

There are no independent contractors in education. We are each part of a school district, part of a school, part of a department or grade-level team, part of a committee, and so much more. Our successes and our failures as a member of a school team do not happen in isolation, therefore, we should not choose to be isolated in any aspect of our job. Teaching can be done when you close your door and keep to yourself, but it can be done so much better when you embrace the teams you belong to.

Three things tend to inhibit our ability to truly be collaborative with our peers; the first is our love of autonomy; the second is varying degrees of self-awareness; and the third is a lack of understanding as to why we collaborate in the school setting. All three are major players leading to isolation or stagnation because of limited collaboration.

AUTONOMY

Autonomy is not about ego or arrogance. Autonomy is something that nearly everyone enjoys and seeks out. In fact, Daniel Pink's research on motivation shows that autonomy drives motivation, performance, and job satisfaction. It's natural to want autonomy and control over your work, but collaboration is also important when working on a project or more importantly when operating as part of a team. Here are a few tips that can help you reconcile your desire for autonomy with the need to collaborate.

First, and this is good practice for all levels of collaboration, establish clear roles and responsibilities. Essentially, create a system where everyone has roles and responsibilities and within that role you have great autonomy to do what you think is best. Structure is built, but within that structure, variability and freedom exist. In theory, this is how all effective schools are structured.

Next, communication is essential when asked to give up some autonomy for the greater good. With a decrease in accountability, everyone on the team must stay hyper informed about the mission, vision, and outcomes of any task that is being tackled together. The key to effective collaboration is the ability to help each other grow.

Communication flowing in both directions means that all people working together must be willing and able to receive positive and negative constructive feedback and then adjust their practices accordingly. Negative feedback always gives the ego a twinge of pain, but with every piece of negative feedback you receive, a nugget of truth can be unearthed to ensure you stay unfinished.

Lastly, if you love autonomy and are trying to figure out how to be a great teammate, please take the time to set boundaries. While collaboration is important, it's also important to set boundaries and establish some level of autonomy so that agency exists at the team level and sanity can persist at the individual level.

This often looks like setting aside some time to work independently or setting guidelines for when and how team members can provide feedback. The bottom line is that any educator reading this should not feel bad for wanting to protect some level of autonomy within their work. That said, no educator should use their desire for autonomy as an excuse to not engage productively with their colleagues or to be a bad teammate.

What about having to work with people whose values don't align with your own or who don't demonstrate a willingness or desire to be part of a team? That has been one of the hardest things to navigate over the years for so many in our profession. There also can be some competition and one-upping of each other, something that may be amplified more now that we exist in an Instagram-worthy culture where we curate our experiences to create this beautiful (but unrealistic) showcase of our lives.

Aside from self-governance and self-regulation, this construct would have to be addressed in some more formal way. Ultimately, overcoming issues of varying personal values or unwillingness to be part of a team comes back to modeling who we want our students to be. In their world and their futures, they will encounter others with different values, and they may or may not want to collaborate with them. It's our responsibility to get over our own issues and model for them what we hope they will become. We should expect and demand this from one another.

SELF-AWARENESS

Each of us brings a unique set of skills, personality traits, and perspectives to any team that we are a part of. This sentence in and of itself is not controversial in any way. The issue, however, is that many people are unaware of exactly what they are bringing to the table. Without a great deal of work to increase self-awareness, almost everyone brings blind spots to the table with them. These blind spots may radically inhibit your ability to collaborate or even worse, your ability to be a great teammate.

To illustrate this point further, we will share a quick story. A colleague and friend of ours (who we will call Jim) was successful in his career and in his community by any imaginable measure. He did some work on self-awareness including the use of personality profiles. In Jim's case, he had used, and now swears by, the Enneagram personality profile.

In Jim's reading of his personality profile, it was noted that his personality type can tend to come off as condescending in meetings. He had worked with the same team for about four years, and they had a strong and open relationship. That nugget of potential condescension sat with him because it was antithetical to everything he was trying to build. So, at the close of his next meeting, Jim decided to ask his team if he came across as condescending in meetings.

In his words, the room turned into a group of bobbleheads. He said that he was equal parts proud that they were willing to be honest with him, but also saddened that this had gone on for years without anyone actively intervening to help him grow. At that moment, Jim had two choices. He could honor the feedback and try to improve or go back to having a massive blind spot that went without intervention.

Of course, as an unfinished educator Jim immediately made subtle and significant changes to his behavior in meetings. He noticed changes rapidly. It seemed that he was invited to more meetings and that his team finally started to participate openly and passionately as he had hoped for throughout his tenure with this group.

The point is that we simply bring all of us wherever we go. While we are collaborating, we bring with us a litany of personality and other traits that either help us to collaborate and make us a great teammate or serve to make the process harder. With increased self-awareness we can continue to build upon our strengths and work hard to mitigate our weaknesses in our efforts to improve and stay unfinished.

COLLABORATION

We all have things to learn from our colleagues, and they have things to learn from us. When we acknowledge that fact, it ultimately leads to better collective wisdom, better ideas, and, most importantly, better outcomes for all kids. The whole premise of the unfinished teacher is truly becoming the next version of yourself.

Often, it's best accomplished through working with others and contributing as a team member. Many studies have shown the value of deliberate, collaborative work–teamwork. Merely meeting with others does not make you part of a team.

The point of collaboration is almost always to create a solution to a problem and/or to improve current practices. When that is distilled to its rawest form, the point of collaboration is to find the most productive ways to change our behaviors. Collaboration that leads to stagnated behavior simply means that the people involved in the collaborative process must have decided that the results currently being achieved are precisely the desired results.

The most common form of collaboration in schools, by name, is that of the Professional Learning Community (PLC) popularized by the late, great Rick DuFour. DuFour reinforced the above point brilliantly and directly:

> The fact that teachers collaborate will do nothing to improve a school. The purpose of collaboration can only be accomplished if the professionals engaged in collaboration *are focused on the right things*. DuFour et.al, LBD, 91

Based on this premise, the four questions of the PLC have become common vernacular in American schools teaching educators how to collaborate and how to focus on the right things.
The four questions are as follows:

1. What do we want students to know and be able to do?
2. How will we know if they know it and are able to do it?
3. What will we do if they do not know it?
4. What will we do if they do know it?

To answer these questions with fidelity, passion, and purpose is to collaborate. To truly collaborate on these questions, there must be a true willingness to change some of the current adult behaviors. To figure out which behaviors to change both as a collaborator and as an educator, there must be self-awareness and a willingness to sacrifice a degree of autonomy for the greater good of the students and school that are being served.

It's possible that a teacher who wants to be a great team player is not considered one. They tried to discuss and share new ideas, co-plan lessons and units, and work together to solve problems, but teacher collaboration means different things to different people. In our ideal world, teacher teams are focused on the four questions and the members professionally respect and care for one another. In the next section on coaching, we identify how peers and supervisors or guides and coaches can help level set or reset teamwork.

COACHING

We had the opportunity to work with a highly successful young teacher (who we will call Sammi). Sammi had accomplished a tremendous amount at a young age. She continued to receive awards and accolades and was highly respected among her peers in the school where she worked and, in the region, at large. She was one of the few young teachers who had the apparent moxie to not only hold her own in a tough school environment but also thrive.

While Sammi was the favorite teacher of many of her students at Westside Prep, there was one problem. While her peers respected her, very few seemed to like her, and nobody wanted to collaborate with her. This realization confounded Sammi, and she confided this information to her coach. The coach continued to ask questions to gain understanding of the situation, but also in hopes of helping Sammi consider the situation from different perspectives. As the coaching continued, Sammi started to understand that the very things that made her successful in the classroom might be making it harder for her in the faculty lounge.

Sammi learned that her default behavior was to be direct, assertive, and to take control of potentially chaotic situations. This was exactly what was needed in her classroom and within her department but was very off-putting to her colleagues. Through her work with her coach, she learned that her default behavior and personality characteristics did not have to lead to how she interacted with her colleagues.

Her coach helped her realize that she was not her personality. She had a choice and could modify her behavior to become a better teammate. She was willing and able to take proactive steps forward because a coach was willing to ask her questions. Before Sammi unlocked this level of self-awareness, she treated the entire world like a nail because her only tool was a hammer.

After gaining understanding of this, she was able to fundamentally shift how she treated others and became not only a respected teacher, but also a valued colleague. Sammi was not finished; like us all, she was unfinished.

Every great instructional, executive, or leadership coach begins with the mindset that the answer is already within the person they are serving. Masterful coaches can help reframe situations for the people they are working with so that the coachee (the person being coached) can gain a different perspective on the same situation they have been working through individually.

More importantly, great coaches ask great questions. Coaches are not concerned with the outcome of the situation that they are working through with their coachee. Coaches are concerned with helping the coachee understand why they continue to run into the problems that they have and to help them analyze how to respond in such situations.

This understanding is what will ultimately lead to increased self-awareness and eventually to peak performance. A great coach helps someone take complete ownership of their situation. In life, many of the situations that educators are thrust into are not their fault. However, once involved, there is a personal responsibility to help create a solution. Unfinished educators know that simply because something is not their fault it does not absolve them of their responsibility to try and improve the situation.

While coaching is not universally available to all educators, our belief is that when someone is ready to be coached, they will find the appropriate person to help fill that void. As part of being unfinished teachers, we believe that every teacher and every leader deserves a coach and hope you will seek one out and advocate for yourself and others within your district.

CHANGES IN PERSONNEL

In the combined seventy-five-plus years we have been working in education, we have worked with thousands of people. We have seen folks thrive, while others have moved from school to school or from district to district or have left education altogether. Rarely do people lose jobs over their professional competencies. Often people lose their jobs because of their inability to be a good teammate.

When it comes to curriculum and content, we generally know "our stuff. "Rarely do people lose their jobs due to misconduct. We all know those people, and we know those stories because they stick in our heads. However, those situations are very few and far between.

Most personnel changes happen because people cannot get along well enough with others. In the medical profession, they call it bedside manner. In education, it takes the shape of friction among the grade-level team or the department. It looks like gossip, distrust, and competition instead of collaboration.

It looks like an inability to forge relationships with students, parents, colleagues, administrators, and community members. It reeks of rigidity, perhaps also insecurity and fear.

No administrator wants turnover. Firing is not a strategy. All schools benefit from the longevity and consistency of their teaching staff.

When this is happening well, people spend their entire careers in a particular place. While it is undoubtedly the job of administration to constantly be working to influence climate and culture, the individuals within the building are those who create a workplace environment that retains the highest quality educators.

CHAPTER SUMMARY

We all need to accept our role as unfinished teachers to continually work on trusting relationships with everyone around us. There are new relationships to build every year, and nearly every day. It is possible to do this work in a silo, but the very best teachers and thereby the very best schools have cultures where people *choose* to work together on behalf of the students and community they serve.

The bedrock of all productive relationships is trust. Trust cannot exist without high character and competency. If there is a challenge to form trusting relationships within a school, department, or team there is almost universally one of the following core components missing: honesty, reliability, empathy, confidentiality, or personal accountability. Thus, this is a moment to look in the mirror.

If you are reading this and cannot think of a single productive, high functioning team that you are a part of, ask yourself if there is one of the above core components of trust that you are not embodying at this stage of your professional career.

To be the type of teammate that helps create such an environment, the best teachers are also the best teammates. It allows you to join committees, help drive decision-making, and support those around you. It allows you to mentor, coach, and support those who previously did (and maybe still do) the same for you.

Tomorrow Takeaways

- Being a good teammate will involve a slight loss in autonomy and require a high level of self-awareness, and high-quality collaborative conversations will ultimately lead to changes in adult behavior.
- While you were selected and hired to work with students, a tremendous part of your work time will be working with colleagues. Be a good teammate, and everyone will benefit.
- The entire concept of Professional Learning Communities (PLCs) is based upon teamwork (focused, deliberate, thoughtful, and intentional teamwork).
- Coaching is what you do every day. It's also what you (and we all) need to receive every day as well.
- Being a great teammate means you are worthy of giving and receiving trust.

Reflection Questions

- What is the last bit of feedback you received that helped you become a teammate and how did you seek out that information?
- What adult are you investing in right now without any pretense of needing anything in return?
- How are you actively working to improve your awareness and eliminate blind spots that may lead to you being a difficult teammate?
- Who do you currently coach and who serves as your coach?

2

Awareness

"If you don't know who you truly are, you'll never know what you really want."
—Roy T. Bennett

Guiding Question: Who are you, and who are your students?

A Teacher Said to Us: "I have a hard time connecting with my students. Our backgrounds are very different and I don't know if I don't understand them, or they don't understand me."

OUR LIVED EXPERIENCES

One of the most powerful quotes discussing self-awareness is "I bring all of me wherever I go." It is an important reminder that, as human beings, we are incredibly complex and that there are layers to our personality, behaviors, values, and beliefs which either directly or subtly impact every interaction we have with others. To distill that down to a more educational example, as teachers you bring all of you into the classroom every single day.

At any given point in our lives, each of us, as a person and as an educator, is the sum of all our experiences and our knowledge up until that point. Two things should stand out when considering that statement.

First, we are never done growing because we will continue to gain knowledge and experience. We are indeed unfinished. The second key element to consider is equally as important, but less evident. While we are constantly changing and evolving; we are never the experiences and the knowledge that we do not possess. At least not yet. That's the exciting part of embracing the idea of being unfinished.

Who are you as an individual on this journey called teaching? And who are you as an unfinished teacher, becoming the next version of yourself? We're thrilled to join you on your personal and professional journey!

THE PATH TO SELF-AWARENESS

It might be easy to think of self-awareness as one simple question: Who am I? However, it shouldn't be that simple and cannot be that simple. The unfinished teacher also asks who am I not? Who do my students need me to be? Where are the gaps in my knowledge and experiences? And maybe most importantly, how do I bridge those gaps?

On the path to self-awareness, there are many opportunities for us to get to know "who we are." There are personality tests we can use, and there are self-assessments about our learning approaches, conflict tolerance, leadership, etc. There are rubrics and all sorts of self-help types of resources for us to conduct some self-review.

For the unfinished teacher, striving to become the next version of oneself, the path to self-awareness is part of the joy of learning, growing, changing, iterating, and reiterating. In this chapter, and in this book, we are asking you to focus on yourself. Focus on your "why" and your "who." Why are you on this awesome yet challenging path in education? Who are you becoming as you live, lead, experience, and grow?

On your path to self-awareness, you'll do your own introspective thinking and checking and reflection (as we start to describe in the next section). You will also learn about who you are via the perceptions of your primary stakeholders, your students, and their families. Awareness is the concept we're starting the book with on our collective journey toward being the next version of ourselves.

REFLECTION

The ability to look back, analyze and evaluate your own reactions and behaviors must be a key cog in the process of increasing one's own understanding of themselves. Reflection is a prerequisite and the definite price of admission to doing any work that helps to increase your understanding of self.

Unfortunately, while reflection is necessary, it is inherently limited. Think back to your first weeks, months, and years in the classroom. Most likely the desire to be amazing for your students was absolutely driving the action taking place inside and outside of the classroom.

If you are like many new teachers, any time that the mind had to be idle, the day *that was* replays in your head. Every decision you made, interaction you had, approach you deployed, were all analyzed in that downtime you had because you wanted to continue to learn, stay unfinished, and provide the best possible instruction for your kids.

Thankfully in teaching there is great camaraderie among the faculty! Even if you are reflecting alone, you will not be alone for long as your buddy teacher or your neighbor or any number of your teacher friends and colleagues will be with you throughout the days and weeks. Often the awareness of and the engagement with one another helps us get through all times, both good and challenging.

Consider what those conversations in your own head would sound like now if you are an experienced teacher. Or, if you are still in the dawn of your career, imagine the difference in your own reflective practices when you are in year ten, fifteen, or twenty in the classroom. Our ability to reflect and deeply analyze the events of the day is proportional to not only our self-awareness, but also to the level of understanding we have of the greater educational context as well.

To what degree do we have awareness of self as well as awareness of the world around us? Do we become more aware as we develop greater empathy for others? Do we become more aware as we understand ourselves better? These are questions worthy of review, reflection, and reconsideration as we develop and evolve.

The depth of someone's awareness is dependent on three things:

- Their willingness to ask deeper questions that require higher levels of critical thinking.
- The experience and/or depth of knowledge to support their processing of the question.
- The appropriate context, whether internally provided or externally supported, to sustain internal discourse that helps someone potentially arrive at new or different understandings.

So, when you find time to reflect, do you stop at whether students were well-behaved or if the lesson "went well?" Or do you truly reflect on whether you met your students where they were and if you truly met their unique needs? Until we have a depth of understanding that allows us to ask and answer the questions of what, why, and how, it becomes difficult to have a clear understanding of who we are as teachers. More importantly, it becomes nearly impossible to strategically plot out who we want to become.

PROFESSIONAL LEARNING

Let's imagine that you are planning to teach a lesson about Mount Rushmore. Let's start with self-awareness. If you don't know much about Mount Rushmore, you can go visit it in person or virtually. You can pick up a book. You can search about it online. You can talk to people who have been there. Once you have that knowledge or that firsthand experience, you can tell others about it, you can teach others about it, and you can make connections to other knowledge and experiences.

Now let's bridge this to your students. You can teach students that Mount Rushmore is in South Dakota and that it features George Washington, Thomas Jefferson, Abraham Lincoln, and Theodore Roosevelt. With additional knowledge and context, we can also teach students that the Lakota Sioux view Mount Rushmore as a reminder of the loss of sacred land that was promised to them by our government and then later taken away when gold was discovered there.

That was likely never taught to you (or any of us) in school. Where are your blind spots in your curriculum? What biases do you knowingly or unknowingly bring into the classroom? How do you look to teach topics in a way that is culturally responsive?

So, in this example, how do you grow your own self-awareness to be the teacher your students need you to be? What professional development do you need? How do we identify the things we don't know and where do we seek that knowledge, strategies, and understandings?

There are layers to everything. Who are you and who do your students need you to be? When reflecting on our performance in the classroom, there must be an awareness in terms of what high-quality instruction looks like. The combination of understanding who *you* are with the understanding of what high-quality instruction looks like is what unlocks the potential for greatness and leads to a natural commitment to remaining unfinished because of the incredible success that will be experienced.

When it comes to professional learning, ideally your school system allows for some type of choice based or individualized professional development/learning opportunities. In our experiences, we have noticed some awesome, whole-group professional development. But there are so many in our organizations for whom the whole-group approach may not allow them to truly grow, learn, or benefit each time.

In addition to adult or staff professional learning and development, so much of who we are as individual educators comes through in our interactions with students and parents. The most beneficial professional learning will resonate with us as individuals and professionals who are on this continual journey of discovery and growth.

YOUR STUDENTS

As you focus on yourself and your own quest, you can embrace becoming the next version of yourself. In what ways are you aware of how you are creating conditions that are helping others, notably your students, discover the next versions of themselves? Ideally, in your classroom (office, etc.) you are creating conditions every day for each child that help support growth, achievement, discovery, and success.

The school buildings we frequent every day were built for the students, not for the adults. If this is true, how do we as teachers impact the physical spaces and the learning environments in such ways that promote student self-awareness and growth, just like our own?

While we dive into topics including curriculum, technology, equity, being a great teammate and others, later in the book, we start with awareness to help ground us in a foundation of focus and self-discovery that can be transferred to the students we serve too.

BLIND SPOTS

Everyone has blind spots. There are areas of behavior, performance, or personality that may be negatively impacting our success, and we have no idea what those may be. Feedback is essential to understanding and addressing our blind spots. As James Clear said, "The trick to viewing feedback as a gift is to be more worried about having blind spots than hearing about them."

Feedback isn't good or bad. All feedback is good. The reality is that some feedback is easy to hear, and some is more difficult to hear. But it's always better to know than not to know.

Automobiles are now equipped with sensors that call attention to our blind spots while driving. Unfinished teachers realize they have blind spots and through various efforts, make a conscious act to mitigate these blind spots in their work, personal lives, and overall being.

The issue with promoting feedback as a key mechanism to increase awareness is that many people may be reading this and thinking they have little control over this. Some teachers do not have administrators that observe them and provide feedback. Others have no access to coaching or support services and may be reading this and thinking they are stuck right now.

One genre of tools that is seldom used in this capacity that has had a great impact are personality profiles. Some people are fully engaged with this type of tool while others reject them as "pop psychology." Even if you are a naysayer, understanding personality archetypes often allows people to see themselves through a different lens than they did before. Each time we do that, we can choose to stay unfinished.

If you are intrigued by personality profiles, market leaders are Enneagram, Myers-Briggs, and DISC. In our opinion, the Enneagram assessment provides the greatest amount of information and resources to find those hidden blind spots of your default personality and helps to provide a deeper understanding of who you are and perhaps why you are. This understanding helps to peel back one more layer of the onion which metaphorically represents the complexity of human psyche and behavior.

Finding or discovering blind spots need not be restricted to formal observations and interactions. You should also create and enter spaces where "real talk" from colleague observations will lend oneself to open discovery and awareness. Opportunities both formal and informal will help us remain unfinished and open to becoming the next versions of ourselves.

AWARENESS PROMOTES EMPATHY

A teacher may never share the same culture and lived experiences as the students in that classroom. In fact, that's impossible. Awareness is all about understanding both who you are and who kids need you to be. The better the understanding of self, the more likely it is that someone will yearn for a deeper understanding of others.

The teachers who take the time to understand why students with Mexican heritage set up las ofrendas for Día de los Muertos and how to support Muslim students while they fast during Ramadan are almost always the teachers that take the time to deeply understand themselves and examine their own values and beliefs.

Until unfinished teachers understand who they are, deeply, it becomes difficult to know what experiences each child brings to the classroom each day and what that means in terms of the changed behavior necessary from the teacher to create a successful classroom. Examples such as this could go on forever, and it's not meant to create guilt in anyone. To learn more about this, we recommend looking into the emerging research around Adverse Childhood Experiences (ACEs).

Vulnerability also plays a huge part here. After all, we have to admit that we don't know everything, and we cannot know everything. We must be willing to acknowledge this, while having the courage to consider things from another's point of view. That's the crux of awareness, being unfinished, and seeking connection.

CHAPTER SUMMARY

The path to any type of personal and professional growth begins with a firm understanding of who one is and where they are on their personal journey. This chapter helps each reader to understand multiple ways they can work to better understand themselves and their individual blind spots, tendencies, and steps they can take to start addressing them.

By discovering who we really are, the freedom to become who we desire to be is unlocked. Can you laugh at your own imperfections? Can you identify yourself in terms of strengths? These are parts of self-awareness that the unfinished teacher will come back to often. How are you doing on your journey to become the next version of yourself?

It starts with you and your own personal and professional self-awareness. The hope of this book is to give readers the tools and motivation they need to move past this form of reflective thinking to unlock the capacity to truly remain unfinished.

Tomorrow Takeaways

- Evaluate your reflective practices and consider if reflection is anything more than just replaying the day's events in your head.
- Find a colleague who will either serve as your formal coach or at least as a critical friend that will help you to see the world through a different lens.
- Strive to identify and attack your blind spots. As a hint—if most of your issues all have seemingly similar context, identify what your default behavior or reaction is typically.
- Take a personality profile or two and see what it asserts about your personality that you may not have known or disagree with. Discuss these findings with your critical friend or people you know, trust, and love. If you are going to take one test, Enneagram is our suggestion.
- Consider empathy you are comfortable deploying in areas where you have a better understanding of the context or of yourself. Work to find the next areas you can expand this strength toward staying unfinished.

Reflection Questions

- What methods do you currently use to increase your self-awareness and how do you judge their effectiveness?
- In what ways are your students different from you? How are you actively trying to bridge that gap so that you can be the teacher they need you to be?

- When you analyze stressful situations, are you able to assess your typical reaction and/or the typical behaviors that led to the stressful situation?
- Evaluate how your level of self-awareness has moved proportionately to your level of knowledge in each area over time. (In areas you have a great depth of knowledge, are you able to better analyze your own performance?)
- When you consider your core values, would your partner, your colleague, or your best friend concur with your assessment?

3

✣

Personal and Social-Emotional Health

When dealing with people, remember you are not dealing with creatures of logic, but with creatures of emotion.

—Dale Carnegie

Guiding Question: In what ways are you taking care of yourself?

A Teacher Said to Us: "I feel burned out. Every year feels more difficult than the last and I'm not sure I can keep doing this."

CALL TO ACTION

Nobody wakes up in the morning and says, "You know what? I want to feel burned out today." That is never the desired state. This goes for everyone from teachers to business leaders to clergy. Nobody wants the terrible feeling of angst that comes from feeling burned out without any clear path forward.

This is it. This is the call to action. We collectively belong to the best profession in the world. On any given day we have the unique opportunity to change the trajectory of a child's life. However, if our teachers are collectively on the verge of burnout to the point where their personal physical and social-emotional health is in jeopardy, then we must take action.

A study conducted by the National Educators' Association in 2022 noted that 90 percent of teachers felt burned out, leading over half of all teachers to consider exiting the profession earlier than originally intended. This data aligns with a Merrimack College and EdWeek report which noted that under 15 percent of teachers noted that they were "very satisfied" with their jobs.

It would be easy to write this off as a condition caused by the unique circumstances of the pandemic, but the same Merrimack study shows that the sharp decrease in teachers satisfied with their jobs started well over a decade ago. In a 2022 Gallup Poll, participants were asked about how often they felt burned out at work. The most extreme answer possible was "Always/Very Often."

The highest response came from K–12 educators as 44 percent of them chose that option. The next highest groups were:

- College/University Employees—35 percent
- Professional Services—33 percent
- Government Positions—33 percent
- Retail—32 percent
- Healthcare—31 percent
- Law—31 percent

Even though this sense of burnout is highest in our profession, it is prevalent in all professions. Just as more and more seems to be added to the plates of educators, the same can likely be said for all these employee groups. We are not alone.

The issue is that there is no simple solution to this complex problem. Instead, our path forward includes a variety of steps and strategies that detail the changes necessary within the holistic educational system.

For positive outcomes to exist, there must also be an acute awareness that many of the necessary steps forward include taking a deep inward look and not expecting or relying on outside solutions to push us forward. This is what we need to do if we hope to end the daunting cycle of burnout.

TEACHING IS A DEMANDING JOB

Two things can be true at the same time. First, the job is difficult and the weight which is placed on educators should *never* be diminished or questioned. The second is that the job is not going to get easier, and we should be working (at least) equally as hard to develop skills to create more resilience than looking for a magic bullet to make the job demands less stressful.

The bottom line is that there are systematic changes that need to be made to ensure that the profession of education is lifted in society's eyes, that compensation matches the demands and education levels and preparation of the position, and that there is collective effort to improve working conditions for all educators.

While that is all true and leaders must continue to fight that fight, collectively we as educators have a responsibility to ourselves and our families to prioritize our own health and social-emotional well-being. The easiest way it can be distilled down for each person reading this book is: *It's okay not to be okay.* It's just not okay to stay there.

If you are overwhelmed or burned out right now, there should be zero guilt involved in feeling that way. That said, it is *not okay* to stay there. And it is okay to ask for help when you need it. When people feel overwhelmed, it is typically because they do not possess the skills necessary to navigate whatever situation they are encountering which is making them feel that way.

The intent of this chapter is not to downplay the stress or rigors of the job. Instead, it is to give each individual teacher some ideas and tools they can use to chart their own path forward. The first step in doing so is to understand what causes burnout and feelings of being overwhelmed to settle over us in the first place.

CAUSES OF BURNOUT

There are many factors that can contribute to teacher burnout. Unsurprisingly, many of these factors are inverted from what we know from Daniel Pink's research creates motivation. The three core factors of motivation, per Pink, are the ability to work on something that has purpose, to do that work with autonomy, and to be able to continually grow as an individual as that work progresses.

Given that, it is clear how antithetical those conditions are to what are some significant causes of teacher burnout:

- High workload: Teachers often must juggle multiple tasks and responsibilities, including preparing lessons, grading assignments, and participating in meetings and professional development. This can be overwhelming, especially if a teacher is not given enough time to complete these tasks. Moreover, when these tasks either do not seem aligned or, worse, seem to contradict the primary goals of directly serving students which serves to provide purpose for teachers, burnout and and a sense of being overwhelmed can settle upon any teacher.
- Lack of support: Teachers may feel isolated or unsupported if they do not have access to resources or if they do not feel like they have the backing of their administration or colleagues. Teachers desire the ability to grow in their craft—this is a natural function of humans.

One of the best things we can do for ourselves is to create a vision for the future and to find and/or provide support for ourselves and others as we traverse the path forward.

- Lack of autonomy: Teachers may feel frustrated if they do not have control over their classrooms or if they are not able to make decisions that affect their students. The same way that children can suffer from overprogramming of their schedules by well-intentioned parents, the same holds true for many working in our educational systems. The best-laid plans of creating supports and programs to influence student outcomes can serve to decrease the autonomy practitioners feel inside their own classrooms and thus decrease the joy of the job.
- Lack of recognition: Teachers may feel undervalued if they do not receive recognition or appreciation for their work. The best recognition is always authentic and specific and oftentimes spontaneous. The best resource we have consulted in learning how to better do this is the book *The Power of Moments* by Chip and Dan Heath. This book gives the what, the why, and the how of providing outstanding recognition for peers, colleagues, and employees.
- Stressful work environment: Teachers may experience high levels of stress if they work in a challenging or chaotic school environment. Teachers are amazing at teaching! When everything else muddies the waters and distracts or does not allow our teachers to use their superpower, we run a risk of creating an environment that supports burnout instead of preventing it. Leaders must do better, and teachers must focus on controlling the controllable to provide order to a potentially stressful environment.
- Personal issues: Teachers, like all people, may experience personal problems that can affect their ability to do their job effectively. The best example is to consider how well someone performs at eight o'clock in the morning if they had a disagreement with a friend or family member before leaving for work that day. The answer is simple, and it is always worse than if no argument occurred. This makes sense at the micro-level, but also must be considered at the macro-level. Many teachers are working through their own personal traumas and that is adversely affecting their ability to bring all of themselves to the school environment.

Teacher burnout is a plague impacting our schools at a near-catastrophic level. It is necessary for every educator to take agency in ensuring their own social-emotional well-being and to aid and assist in supporting their colleagues. We must all take ownership in being part of our own paths forward. As we improve our own physical and social-emotional health, we will guide the way for our colleagues to do the same.

For ultimate success, there must be a two-pronged approach to address burnout and a sense of feeling overwhelmed. To move forward, we must remember that we are *whole* people. In much the same way there is an educational focus on the whole child, we need to deploy that approach to ourselves. Thus, we will discuss how to move forward by focusing on both our personal well-being and our social-emotional well-being.

PHYSICAL HEALTH

We simply cannot pour from an empty cup. While this quip is frequently used, it is also a bit misunderstood. Most people internalize this as a social-emotionally focused saying. While it could be used in that way, it is much simpler to think of it in terms of our physical health. If you are unwell, it is going to be impossible to serve your students well.

More importantly, however, is the fact that your family and friends (and you as an individual) deserve and need you to take care of yourselves. If you are sick, please take a sick leave day—rest and get healthy. You are entitled to rest and recover.

This can be as simple as making sure to get normal and regular annual medical checkups, visit the Employee Assistance Program when your mental health demands it, exercise, and eat right. The issue when discussing physical health is that it is very clear and easy to understand what should be done, but it is hard to consistently execute those things with fidelity.

Our desire is to make staying healthy as simple as possible for you. We will do so through an acronym below, but the bottom line can be summed up in four absurdly direct sentences.

- Eat less, move more.
- Eat to live, do not live to eat.
- Know your data. Your cholesterol, blood pressure, and weight (among many other factors) should always be known and monitored.
- Anything in excess is *usually* not good for you in the long term.

SEEDS—A SIMPLE WAY TO STAY HEALTHY

In *The Unfinished Leader*, we identify an acronym for staying healthy. To maintain the necessary health and wellness to perform at your best you must:

- **Sleep**—Commit to getting seven to nine hours per night. While many people have become accustomed to functioning on less than seven hours of sleep, that does not mean that it is healthy.
- **Eat**—Eat to live, do not live to eat. Consume the calories necessary per day to maintain, gain, or lose weight. Sounds easier than it is and please know that collectively we struggle with this as well. The simple step of using any number of apps to count your caloric intake is a great way to realize your blind spots. Two trouble areas for many people are the snacks consumed after arriving at home, before dinner, after dinner, and before bed. Analyzing those calories may help you to see a clear path forward when it comes to your own weight and physical well-being.
- **Exercise**—Elevate your heart rate for at least twenty minutes every day. This is one that most people dramatically overcomplicate. To work toward becoming healthier and more physically fit, just focus on getting the heart rate up for at least twenty minutes per day. This is likely not going to get you in swimsuit model shape or have you ready to run a marathon, but it is the foundation for healthy living. The best part is that this can be done with zero equipment, inside or out, with others or by yourself. We all can make this change immediately. It may also be as simple as standing more often (many people are getting "stand up" desks to help them with this).
- **Drink**—Guidelines shift based on gender, weight, and level of activity, but a good general rule is to consume *at least* eight glasses of water per day. Different people recommend different strategies, but the earlier in the day water is drunk, the less it will interrupt sleep patterns. If you drink most of your water at night, your sleep will be disrupted with frequent bathroom visits. Thus, we suggest you frontload your water intake.
- **Social-Emotional Connectedness**—One of the best things we can do for our physical health is to be around people we love. To be clear, this is not suggesting that mingling with friends of friends or neighbors you barely know will do the trick. This is a reminder that being around those people with whom you have deep loving relationships is a way to positively impact not only your mental health but also your physical well-being.

The key to personal, physical health is focusing on it. So many teachers are literally exhausted due to giving all they have to the students, the profession, and to one another that they unintentionally neglect themselves. It's critical that there begins to be a collective understanding of the value of health and wellness as individuals. Said as plainly as possible, taking care of yourself is not selfish, it's essential.

While physical health and well-being may be easier to see with the naked eye than social-emotional health, having one without the other will ultimately lead to problems. The intent of this section of the book is to provide tangible solutions that anyone can employ to begin to move the needle for themselves when feeling burned out or overwhelmed.

As a disclaimer, there are significant mental and emotional concerns that impact many educators. These tips and techniques may not be valid for someone who is in a true crisis. Please note that any suggestions here are not intended to serve as substitutes for feedback from mental health professionals.

GRATITUDE

Gratitude has been shown to have a positive impact on mental health and well-being. When people focus on what they are grateful for, they are more likely to experience positive emotions and reduce negative ones such as anxiety and depression. This is because gratitude helps shift attention away from negative thoughts and emotions toward positive ones.

A common practice among the three authors is to frequently write or communicate messages of gratitude. These messages not only spread thanks and recognition to the person receiving the message, but also play a wonderful role in helping the person sending the message. While sending positive messages and making phone calls to students and their families is a great idea, consider sending a message of gratitude to the parents of your mentor teacher, or to the spouse of your grade-level teammate!

Spread positive messages and make gratitude the norm. Research has shown that people who regularly practice gratitude are more likely to have better mental health, including lower levels of stress and greater life satisfaction. They also tend to have stronger social connections and are more resilient in the face of adversity.

Harvard psychologist Shawn Achor wrote *The Happiness Advantage* in 2010. In this book, he drew on original research "including one of the largest studies of happiness ever conducted—and worked in boardrooms and classrooms across forty-two countries, . . . Achor shows us how to rewire our brains for positivity and optimism to reap the happiness advantage in our lives, our careers, and even our health."

Expressing gratitude and focusing on positive psychology can take many forms, such as keeping a gratitude journal, expressing appreciation to others, or simply taking time to reflect on the positive things in one's life. The key to leveraging gratitude to improve your own mental health and social-emotional well-being is that the thoughts and messages of gratitude should be as specific as possible.

To explain, instead of thinking about being grateful for your children, think about how grateful you are that your nine-year-old makes their own bed, brushes their teeth without frequent reminders, and loves "Dad jokes." Specificity matters—both for the person expressing gratitude and those receiving the message.

Would you prefer to receive a card from a colleague that says, "Thanks for always being there for me" or "Thanks for making me laugh yesterday when I was beating myself up over a rough lesson?" Both are good—but the latter will stick in your memory and be more impactful. Ultimately, don't be angry when you don't receive gratitude. Instead, find joy in showing gratitude to others.

Every time people hear a certain song, they immediately think of something specific like football on Friday evenings. Another song may bring someone back to their college days or their first dance with their spouse. Music, like many other things, can trigger an emotional response from us as human beings.

Knowing that there are triggers to positive emotion, such as music, extrapolate that to the work environment. It's likely that at one point (and hopefully still), we were all deeply in love with the idea of influencing the next generation of students. Identifying the unique things that brought us joy in that pursuit and then intentionally and systematically recreating those experiences will benefit your mental well-being.

RECLAIMING YOUR WHY

Whether you are in education as a calling, as a profession, as a job, as a career, as a stop on your journey, it's critical to know and "live" your why/purpose. When people experience burnout, overwhelm, or social-emotional angst when it comes to their job, they lose their purpose or their why.

Here are five quick steps you can take to reclaim your why:

1. Reflect on your values: What do you believe about yourself, your profession, and your students? How can you ensure your behaviors reflect your values?
2. Identify your strengths: Think about your skills and talents and how you can apply them to your life and work. Are you intentional about leveraging your superpowers each day? None of us are good at everything, but we are all good at something.

3. Set goals: Our brains love to pursue outcomes. Simply doing the work is not as motivating as doing the work to create a better outcome for someone else or for yourself.
4. Act: We cannot think our way through burnout. We must act and continue to put one foot in front of the other until we start to make progress.
5. Practice self-reflection: Oftentimes burnout and overwhelm come from not realizing how far we have come in our journey. Understanding how much we have grown and impacted the growth of others helps us to identify our why and continue pushing ourselves in that direction.

CHAPTER SUMMARY

We cannot serve others when we are struggling ourselves. Whether the origin of that struggle is physical, mental, or social-emotional, we have a responsibility to ourselves and those we serve to continue to invest in ourselves as much as we invest in those around us.

This chapter outlines strategies that can be used to move ourselves from the brink of burnout back to reclaiming our why and thriving in the profession. In the spirit of staying unfinished, we must *never* stop investing in ourselves and our own health. By taking care of ourselves, we create the pathway to better take care of others.

Tomorrow Takeaways

- You cannot pour from an empty cup. You must take care of yourself to take care of others.
- Systemically we must tackle core issues in education, but individually we cannot wait for someone else to make our jobs more joyful. We must look inward.
- What causes burnout is often antithetical to what causes motivation. We must work to create more autonomy, purpose, and the ability to move toward mastery in our professional lives.
- Practice SEEDS to improve your physical well-being.
- Practicing gratitude, reclaiming your why, and finding your triggers of joy will help to move you away from a state of burnout or a sense of feeling overwhelmed.

Reflection Questions

- What would happen if you took extreme ownership of your level of joy and happiness at work and worked passionately to reignite your why?
- What would it take for you to make your physical health a priority? Is it possible for you to do so without an emergency or a tragedy?
- How long do you think it would take to handwrite a card of gratitude to someone as the very first and very last thing you did at work each day? How do you think that would impact your own level of joy and satisfaction?

4

Financial Health and Wellness

Try to save something while your salary is small; it's impossible to save after you begin to earn more.

—Jack Benny

Guiding Question: Are you deliberately aware of your annual financial health? And if you aren't—why not?

A Teacher Said to Us: "My spouse and I are always stressed about money and about our kids. That stress impacts my relationships with others and my ability to work the way I want to, and it affects my physical health."

REMINDERS

There are two things that happen frequently as a district leader that are stark reminders why this chapter is of the utmost importance for all educators to read. The first is helping someone through their potential retirement earnings from the state-supported system only for the individual to realize that they are unable to retire when they want or, sometimes even more sadly, how they wanted to. The sadness of this event is multiplied because oftentimes it is entirely avoidable with minimal proactive planning.

The second is when someone realizes in the middle of their career that this is no longer the profession that stirs their soul only to realize that they are too dependent upon the state-supported retirement and too far along in their career to make a change. This phenomenon known as the "golden handcuffs" of state-supported retirement is not something that we want any educator to feel is dictating their actions or life choices.

There is a "bonus," third part of financial planning that your authors are becoming more aware of as we get older. If you have a family, you might need to think about the future cost of college or other postsecondary education. You might need to think about the future cost of weddings. Even if you don't have or don't plan to have a family, you will still need to think about the future costs of home repair, car repair, and other unexpected costs associated with life in general.

MONEY 101

When you pour water into any vessel, it will always take the shape of that vessel. The same is true of our money. When we pour money into our bank accounts, our lives seem to adjust accordingly. No matter what we earn in any given year, we always seem to find a way to spend it. More money—new car. More money—new apartment, larger house, new clothes, more nights out. And unfortunately, we often find a way to spend even more than we have. Thanks, credit cards!

In the same manner in which time fills the time allotted it, our lifestyles expand and contract based upon the money earned. While this seems like an oversimplification, money either controls us or we control our money. There really is no in-between, and there is no better time to start than right now to plan and consider your own financial health and wellness.

To make matters worse, financial concerns are always one of the highest stressors in people's lives and marriages. This is supported year after year in many surveys. Namely, a survey by the American Psychological Association found that money was the most common source of stress in relationships, with 31 percent of respondents citing financial concerns as a significant stressor.

So, clearly, our financial health directly impacts our overall wellness. This is not just anecdotal; there are many studies that have strong correlational results indicating level of financial health contributes to overall longevity. The good news is that we can establish good habits that lead to good outcomes. The truth is that there is no limit to the number of outstanding sources that are available for consultation. Moreover, there are many incredible sources of information that are either free of charge or are as inexpensive as picking up some books from your local bookstore.

One of the major issues with financial stress is that it is absurdly personal. While many people have been through challenges and have real-world experience that would put them in a position of support, too many people are unwilling to be vulnerable enough to share their personal plight—until they reach the point of crisis. Anyone that is struggling right now is not the first person to grapple with financial health, and they won't be the last.

BEGIN WITH THE END IN MIND

Financial health for teachers should be governed by Covey's principle of "beginning with the end in mind" from his bestselling *7 Habits of Highly Successful People*. Teachers who enter the profession in their twenties are not always focused on their future selves thirty to forty years later. While understandable, it is not okay, and as unfinished teachers, we beg that you begin to consider your future self, today.

Far too many educators do not think about their financial health and well-being until they approach retirement. With state-sponsored retirement systems continually pushing the age of retirement further out, individuals must take ownership of their own finances. For context, the retirement age for maximum benefits in Illinois for educators new to the field is age sixty-seven! We have a hard time imagining this as a sustainable strategy when we look at the stressors and the physical and emotional toll being a teacher takes on our colleagues.

If anyone is reading this and thinking that this is not necessary, this financial truth is worth considering. Preparing financially may not ultimately be necessary, but nobody ever regrets giving themselves more financial options or financial freedom—particularly as they continue to age.

This section outlines a few simple strategies that can increase financial literacy and, if necessary, be used to help ease the reliance many people have on their state-supported programs. To be clear, state-supported retirement programs are an amazing perk of being a public educator, but our call to action for each person reading this book is to work diligently to decrease your reliance on those systems.

Without such reliance, educators will have increased financial options throughout their careers and will not feel the burden of the proverbial "golden handcuffs" of the retirement system. To begin, let's start with the absolute basics.

Too often teachers, both new and veteran, are not always fluent in their paycheck. Some people who study every item on a receipt when they are out to dinner are unaware of everything occurring in their own paycheck. Most people know their base salary and any potential stipends for supervision, but they are not always in tune with the other details.

Please schedule time with your human resources department and ask the people who do the payroll to explain your check stub. It's okay to ask. It's very important to know what the deductions are, what the benefits are, and what your paycheck reflects.

There is a myriad of things worth becoming familiar with because each presents a unique opportunity to better your financial standing or minimally provide you with either more control or more options. For example, we encourage each reader to become more familiar with the tax laws of their state, the benefits of long-term savings or retirement planning, or the nuances of how sick days, for example, might be benefit days that can help them decades later with far greater value than not using.

Ask the union representatives to work with the business office to get some financial planners in for "lunch and learn" sessions to share information about these topics with interested parties (you). It's often daunting to start to understand the oddities and complexities of taxes and tax planning, but it will literally pay you dividends if you start this inquiry in your twenties or thirties rather than in your fifties or sixties.

A lack of knowledge in this area can lead people to leave their current district for greener pastures only to find that they made the wrong decision. In preparation for writing this chapter we met with a teacher who left a tenured position where they had great influence over the direction of their department for a new district for a higher salary. This move on its surface seemed to make sense.

The teacher did not realize that the new district did not cover the state-supported pension program and left a better situation for less total compensation. Ouch! Other people make the same mistake when not considering insurance costs and other benefits not typically considered. There is far more to how much you "make" than the base salary alone.

As the quote at the start of this chapter infers, the time to start saving is *now*. It will never be the right time to start taking home less money. Start saving money immediately, even when you don't have a lot to save, and you don't think about the time when you will need this. Given consistent return rates on long-term investments, and the impact and effects of compounding, a pretax deduction of $225 per check starting at age twenty will leave you a millionaire at sixty years old. If you begin with the end in mind, you can do this!

FINANCIAL STRESS

Financial stress manifests in a variety of ways. First and foremost, financial stress is a leading cause of anxiety and depression. Data supporting that is provided below showing just how prevalent this is in the lives of all Americans. Annually the American Psychological Association conducts a Survey of Stress.

Its 2022 survey found that 72 percent of Americans reported feeling stressed about money at least sometime in the prior month. One specific question (below) revealed that 52 percent of respondents stated that financial strain increased over the past year. Only 11 percent of respondents said financial stress decreased.

Among Those Who Say Money Is a Significant Source of Stress

Has financial strain in your household increased, decreased, or stayed the same over the past year?

- Increased 52 percent
- Stayed the same 38 percent
- Decreased 11 percent

Equally as important to the strain finances can play on someone's mental and emotional health, financial stress can negatively impact physical health. A study by the National Institute of Health found that financial stress is associated with higher levels of inflammation in the body, which can lead to a range of health problems, including heart disease, diabetes, and cancer.

Financial stress can lead to relationship problems. Nearly one-third of couples cite financial stress as a key component to relationship stress with their significant other or spouse. While this likely sounds familiar and most people can relate, the question is whether people are taking the proactive steps at their fingertips to gain more control over this segment of their lives.

Lastly, since this book is about education, it is vital to note that financial stress can affect work performance. A survey by the Society for Human Resource Management found that 37 percent of employees reported being distracted by financial worries while at work, and 34 percent said financial stress had a negative impact on their productivity.

The bottom line is that we are each one singular human being. People cannot compartmentalize our stress the way many try to convince themselves it is possible. Simply said, everyone is a better version of themselves when their financial house is in order.

When we focus on financial education, when we address financial health and wellness, and seek guidance, and take advice (and start saving money), we will be healthier overall. If we can acknowledge that stress in general is bad for our health, and financial stress can account for a major source of that stress, getting a financial checkup will not only be healthy for our bank account, but can help to extend our lives. More importantly, being financially healthy will allow a better-quality life throughout the aging process.

SUPPLEMENTAL RETIREMENT INVESTMENTS

Retirement systems will vary from state to state, but what is generally accepted as a truth is that in all states, teachers are generally underpaid and public education is generally underfunded. What is even more scary is that the state-supported pension systems are not considered healthy in most instances.

Healy, Hess, and Nicholson wrote in a Harvard Faculty working paper in 2012 that public pensions in the United States were grossly underfunded by about 730 billion dollars. Ten years later, the Equable Institute estimates that the teacher pension funding gap is 878 billion.

Without trying to be alarmist, teachers who are solely relying on the state-supported system should use this information as their warning light to create an alternative path of retirement savings for themselves. We should plan as if, at some point, the underfunded pensions might not be sustainable.

There are many vehicles to choose from (IRA, Roth IRA, 401(k), 403(b), 457, etc.). We are not financial professionals and therefore you do not want us suggesting one strategy over another. But you do need to speak to a financial professional to understand your options and what best meets your needs.

At this point, the hope is that there is a strong desire to invest in something supplemental to the state system. But, for many reading this, it will sound like an unreachable aspiration. "How can I save money when I barely make enough for my expenses?" Such questions and doubts are eminently reasonable.

However, even saving $25 a paycheck, over time, can grow, compound, and help to create a realistic nest egg for savings and for your financial health in retirement. For instance, an investment of just $25 per check for an entire career will leave someone with well over $100,000 in additional retirement savings. The basic principle of compound interest is the friend of every investor. The average year-over-year investment interest over the past few decades has been approximately 7 percent.

Plainly speaking, it does not matter explicitly with who or how you invest. Find someone you trust and place money aside. The laws of compounding are in your favor. The only rule is this: the earlier you start, the better.

INVEST IN YOURSELF

Educators likely did not go into the profession hoping to get rich. Most went in to serve the children in their community. This is what makes our profession the best in the world—the kindhearted and generous people that we get to serve alongside. Yet we cannot allow kindheartedness to become synonymous with starving. Educators deserve a fair, respectful compensation package for the intense hard work that they do each day.

Given that, it is vitally important that each person reading this book understands that you are the CEO of "Insert Your Name" Incorporated. There are many things that we can all do to cut costs or increase our income at the same time. There are also limitless opportunities outside the world of education that someone can invest in to ensure they are maximizing their earning potential.

Many of us had piggy banks growing up that evolved into change jars, so we *know* how to save money. Do you really need that designer coffee every morning, or could that $5 a day be better served saving for your future? What could you save by cutting out fast food? (That one works for your finances and your physical health!) Could you cut back on drinking, smoking, or any other area of your life where your resources are going to help plan? There are apps for this that can help one with individual tracking too.

We also know that many educators seek employment outside the classroom. We collectively hate the fact that this is something people must do to make ends meet. We also know that this is something some people truly enjoy doing. You might like working part time as a rideshare driver, making and selling crafts online, tutoring students, or any number of secondary employment options.

If that's your thing, either by need or by want, how are you using those resources to support your current and future financial health? As a quick reminder, $225 invested per check throughout your career will likely (given previous compounding history) leave you a millionaire at retirement. The bottom line is this is eminently doable. You also have considerably more control than most people believe.

FINANCIAL LITERACY

Most school districts have someone or a group of people that are designated to help support individual growth in financial literacy, financial planning, and retirement support. Even in cases where your school organization does not, almost all have private partners such as Horace Mann (which was created for educators) or many others that are more than willing to help someone start planning for free.

Just like physical and emotional health and wellness, we submit that financial health and wellness may be just as essential for your efforts. Financial literacy is usually a combination of ten key factors. While the intent of this section is not to go into a deep dive on each, a quick examination of the ten should help you to do a quick self-analysis of your personal financial literacy:

1. Budgeting: Understanding your financial commitments in comparison to the revenue you are bringing in.
2. Saving: Understanding the impact of setting aside money in a repeatable manner.
3. Investing: There are stocks, bonds, mutual funds, certificates of deposit, and many more options. Seek professional guidance on what option works best for your goals and your risk tolerance.
4. Credit: Credit scores help determine an inordinate amount in our own life. Everyone should constantly be aware of their own credit score and what is factoring positively and negatively.
5. Retirement planning: Understanding the importance of retirement savings, inclusive of the perks and benefits that exist in your state and knowing how to set and achieve retirement goals.
6. Financial goals: You may want to target a certain amount in savings, plan to purchase a home, prioritize travel, save for college or weddings, or maybe you want to own a boat. Everyone should have some sort of financial goal they are working toward.
7. Insurance: Understanding the various types of insurance, such as health, life, and property insurance, and knowing how to select the appropriate coverage. This is even more important as people approach retirement and may not have insurance issued by their parents or employer for the first time in their life.
8. Taxes: Understanding the tax system and how to file taxes and knowing how to minimize tax liability. This is more complex than many of the other items in this list and we advise that each person has an accountant they trust.
9. Financial decision-making: Markets and situations change. This speaks to your ability to adjust to the situation at large, but more importantly to your personal situation. If you are living comfortably and then secure a raise, invest more of the raise than the typical percentage invested previously.
10. Consumer awareness: Money can make people do detrimental things. Knowing how to compare prices, avoid scams, and protect personal information when making financial transactions is a skill that you will hopefully never need, but always should have.

CHAPTER SUMMARY

Financial wellness and health simply matter. A strong financial position will frequently reduce the stress on you and your family and will increase positive physical and emotional health.

Many people do not know who to talk to for financial advice. Many people just get a job, take the paycheck, and live their lives without serious planning or financial discipline. We implore you to stop this cycle. It doesn't matter who you ask for help, but you have to ask someone so that you can get started.

In this chapter, information and advice was shared helping to focus the reader on looking far down the road of your career to focus on where everyone wants to be with financial security. This is more than simply wanting to be wealthier for the sake of being wealthier. Financial stress impacts your health. With that in mind, you need to plan for your short-, medium- and long-term financial health.

Finally, we offered some insights on how to get financially literate. As an unfinished teacher, it's equally as important that you focus on the food you eat, the sleep you get, the exercise you do, and the planning you put forth in relation to your financial health and wellness.

Tomorrow Takeaways

- You can combat the stress and fear associated with financial health.
- You can take proactive steps to build financial security.
- The earlier and the more you invest when you are younger will lead to the laws of compounding interest being on your side when you are older.
- The financial health and wellness for you can be planned and taken care of now.
- You can start to put away savings with a small amount of money to begin your path to financial wellness and security.

Reflection Questions

- How much money is enough in supplemental retirement savings when you retire?
- Could you find a way to invest an average of $225 or more every two weeks?
- In what ways are you attuned to your financial health and wellness?
- Do you know who you can call or reach out to for support in terms of financial planning?
- Have you really thought about the intersection between financial wellness, personal growth, and your own overall health?

Teacher Essay 1

Being Self-Aware or "With Great Power Comes Great Responsibility"

Jon Bogie, Fourth-Grade Teacher

I have been collecting comic books since I was a young boy. I was a massive fan of the Fantastic Four and Spider-Man in my early years. The red and blue primary colors of his suit got me hooked. I quickly grew to love the writing of this and all comics. I always loved how superheroes did the right thing, fought the bad guys, and stayed true to their mission.

Over the years, the quote from Spider-Man's Uncle Ben struck me as the pinnacle of his mission, "with great power comes great responsibility." I think this quote sums up something all teachers should keep in their hearts and minds.

Every August, I spend time reflecting on my enormous ability as a teacher to influence my students and help them grow to be the best people they can be. It seems arrogant to think that I would have so much influence. I used to think that way, until former students grew up, reached out to me, and told me how important I was in their lives. It's common for me to get emails from former students telling me about my impact on their lives.

Some of my recent favorites are:

- Being told how my personal nature and the community of our classroom made a difference for him.
- Receiving pictures of mementos from fourth grade, like stress balls and guitar picks I give out as end-of-the-year gifts.
- How playing guitar for the class at the end of the day made them so happy.

When I hear from students that the little and big things I did made an impact on them, it reinforces the idea that everything we do affects our students. That is why I reflect so much on every little detail of my classroom.

To new and young teachers, I would encourage you to spend time reflecting on your students, classroom community, and the impact your actions have on them. You will see some growth in the year they are with you, and if you're lucky, they may come back and visit you when they're older and let you know how important you are to them. Your teaching style will grow, change, and adapt over the years.

Remember to keep evolving your craft to meet the ever-changing needs of your students. As hard as this sounds, it's incredibly satisfying and rewarding, and why we do what we do.

Personal Health

In teaching, it is easy to forget to take care of your physical self. There have been many times when I have forgone working out so I could continue working on lesson plans, grading papers, or coming up with new and fun projects for my class. All those things are crucial and essential for the success of the job. However, they cannot come at the cost of your physical health.

A few years ago, I had a small bump on my knee about the size of the head of a pin. It happened during parent-teacher conferences, and I paid it no heed. By the end of the second day, it had grown a little, but I figured it would just go away. Right after the conferences, I left with my family to attend one of my oldest friends' weddings. It was a five-hour drive, and when we arrived, the little bump was the size of a quarter.

By the next day and the end of the reception, it was the size of a baseball, and I couldn't bend my knee. My wife, my guiding light, drove back home and to our hospital. After a three-day stay with round-the-clock antibiotics, the infection was gone. I even missed a scheduled observation for my evaluation. The lesson I give is to take care of yourself and not put those little things off.

In high school and college, I swam for the varsity teams. As an adult, I have continued this on and off, swimming with the master's teams at Northwestern University. It has kept me in shape and given me a social outlet. Many swimmers were also in education, which made our connection even more substantial. During this time, I was in fantastic physical shape and even took fourth place in the 1,650-yard freestyle at nationals one year.

However, my physical condition changed when I married and had kids. I kept swimming, but it became harder and harder with my responsibilities at home. This is true for a lot of the people on my team. That is life's nature, and we must adapt to the change. So, I joined a health club near my house and went every morning. It worked, and it was great. I was losing the weight I had gained and feeling very good about myself. Then the unthinkable happened, the pandemic. My health club closed, and I had to adapt again. My wife and I are now the proud owners of an elliptical machine, which we are learning to use to keep us in shape.

Staying in good physical condition is critical to being an educator, especially at the elementary level. Whether sitting for circle time or kneeling to tie shoelaces, you need to keep your body in good shape to be the best you can be.

Financial Health and Wellness

I remember the first time I learned what a 403(b) is. I was in my twenties, and it seemed almost silly to think of retirement. I was trying to pay off my educational loans, pay my rent, and pay off my car. Having to save for something thirty-five years away almost seemed wasteful. My father strongly encouraged me to meet with financial advisers to plan my retirement.

After meeting with several people, I agreed to a plan to deduct part of my paycheck and put it into a 403(b) plan. I've always struggled with money, economics, and financial planning. I had to get a tutor for microeconomics in college. I regularly seek the advice of colleagues, family, and friends who know more than me. I learned the benefits of asking for help, especially when you don't know what you're doing.

In 2007, my wife and I bought our first house. We were horrified when the housing market collapsed a few months later, and the value of our new home plummeted. Even though I laid out a plan for retirement, in addition to my pension, I was forced to adapt. Once again, I relied on the advice of family and friends to help me adjust our plans.

Our financial planning was for the long term and could stay afloat until, ten years later, things are back to where they were. New and young teachers must develop a plan for their retirement. Many districts have partnerships with financial firms that can help plan for the day you retire, even though it seems a long way off.

Section 2

INDIVIDUAL AND INTERPERSONAL PROFESSIONAL GROWTH AND CHANGE

Who You Are as a Teacher in the Classroom and Who You Are as a Professional

5

✣

Curriculum, Standards, Assessment, and Data

We have to stop delivering the curriculum to kids. We have to start discovering it with them.

—Will Richardson

Guiding Question: How does an unfinished teacher balance the mandates of the curriculum while infusing their own magic of instruction so that assessment is for learning not of learning?

A Teacher Said to Us: "Sometimes I feel like I'm trying to teach the state standards, sometimes I feel like I'm trying to teach to the next standardized test, and sometimes I feel like I'm trying to teach to the local curriculum. And those things all keep changing. Can't I just teach kids?"

THE ART AND SCIENCE OF TEACHING

For years, it has been debated whether teaching is more of a science or an art. The truth is that it is both. For many amazing teachers, the classroom becomes the venue for their masterful performance art. Anyone who doubts the abundant talent of actors and performers need to look no further than a high school musical or play tryout. In that space, a variety of different actors will read the same lines, and some will make the words come alive and others will simply . . . read the lines.

The content is the exact same, but the product is indescribably different. Teaching is similar in many ways. Just like that high school musical tryout, the teacher may have the guidance of a curriculum or scope and sequence, but the real magic is in the delivery. The same content delivered by a different person and in a different way completely changes the end product for the consumer. The magic that the truly great practitioners bring to a classroom comes from how that teacher takes that curriculum and makes it come alive.

Teachers create that magic in how they meticulously brainstorm, ideate, and then deliver the "script" in unique ways matching their skillset with the needs of the classroom. Done masterfully, the lesson becomes a moment. It becomes something that students will remember forever.

A colleague recalled a lesson from their youth that focused on the importance of elevation in battle. To prove the point, a teacher jumped on a desk and threw racquetballs at the class. The simple concept of an elevated position was the science while the memorable moment was the art. The downside is that when not done thoughtfully, the magic is gone. The lesson becomes one more sit and get opportunity where some students can fall asleep just like a moviegoer or theatergoer during a cinematic flop.

The art is that teaching can be done well. Teachers can create an environment where students are on the edge of their seats and hope that the teacher has a sequel in store for the following day. The pathway to doing so is not easy. Most teachers do not wake up and have the entertainment value of Angelina Jolie or Brad Pitt. There are concrete steps the unfinished teacher can take, however, to help bring their craft alive in a way that makes their classroom both more entertaining and more likely to engage students in meaningful learning.

This is not to suggest that artistic teaching is performance. We do not aim to reinforce a paradigm causing, not solving, educational problems. The following two statements should be untrue:

1. Teachers are active. Students, like moviegoers, are passive.
2. Student engagement is equated with student entertainment. Good teaching is like kids watching a cool show.

Instead, we are aiming to create a paradigm where teachers are recognized for being both artists and scientists in creating conditions for learning for each child every day. There are examples that show some degree of performative art as well as some degree of scientific planning and creating conditions.

Teaching is highly complex. Our aim is to describe and illustrate examples of how the curriculum can be leveraged for student learning. The remainder of this chapter helps to place a bit of the science behind the art necessary to capture, hold, and capitalize on students' attention.

To move forward, the unfinished teacher masters the curriculum, masters how students learn best, and understands the nuances of what students must know and be able to do to be successful.

Being unfinished is always focusing on improving, improvising, and making the most of the daily resources available for each child. To keep charging forward for our kids, an unfinished teacher must have a firm understanding that state tests will change, benchmarks will shift, and modalities will become more complex. These constant modifications can defeat us or spur us forward.

The best among us uses this challenge as the impetus to get better, to improve and to stay current with what is to be taught, how it is to be taught, and how it is to be assessed.

The world is changing at an exponential pace. If schools are to remain relevant, we must embrace change and be part of that process. Teachers who understand and embrace that reality truly know what it means to be an unfinished teacher. Change is to be expected and embraced because it is happening to support the current and future success of our students.

What can be done though, in contrast, if a system is not keeping up with change and the teacher, the innovative teacher, is? How can the unfinished teacher reconcile with an organization stuck in the past or stuck in the mud? This dilemma does not have easy or clear answers, and our raising it here may raise more frustration than action.

What is undeniably true, however, is that those with an unfinished mindset and a willingness to adapt will not only move through changes with a greater level of success but will also likely do so with a greater level of joy. Helping improve the system from within may work. Some may need to improve via another system. These pushes will ultimately lead to overall improvement in the profession.

Curriculum

Given the different dynamics in schools and districts throughout the country (and world), there is a chance that the teacher reading this book may have complete autonomy over the curriculum they teach or no decision-making authority when it comes to what is taught in the classroom. Given this wide range of potential experiences, it is important to highlight both practical and theoretical implications and understandings each unfinished teacher should have.

The argument for a strong, systematized curriculum is that every student in a certain grade level *deserves* the opportunity to access and experience similar learning opportunities and experiences. Visually, it is easiest to imagine the defined curriculum as the skeleton of a class. The skeletons of most humans look pretty similar in terms of the structure and number of bones. Given that, each human being looks very different.

This is where the artistry of the teacher manifests itself. The common vernacular when referring to the curriculum is to refer to it as the "what." The content, the meat and potatoes, the substance of learning content is the curriculum. The curriculum answers the question of what we hope that kids can know and do as a result of taking this course or this grade level.

Sometimes in education, terms are used interchangeably, and that can lead to confusion. The scope and sequence of subject matter is frequently referred to as curriculum. Instead of just answering what we want kids to know and be able to do, the scope and sequence also answers the question of when we want them to demonstrate this knowledge and these skills.

Once standards are developed and adopted, resource providers create tools educators can leverage to help them provide access to the necessary learning for kids. While these resources are incredible, they are not the curriculum.

These are resources designed to help students access the curriculum and to take some of the planning load off teachers as they do everything they can to support kids. This confusion often impedes the growth of teachers. Resources (textbooks, workbooks, websites, etc.) are not the curriculum.

As three superintendents writing a book for teachers, we understand the potential for the conflict of teacher freedom and district mandates. Our professional stance is that the systems must be designed for voice and agency of all involved.

The curriculum should not be so restrictive and limiting that the teacher's artistry is removed. On the contrary, we emphatically believe that teacher voice and agency, along with district and publisher content, must integrate for students, for the profession, and for both the art and science of teaching.

Becoming too rigid, dogmatic, or attached to any curriculum can serve as a blind spot to potential progress for all unfinished teachers and unfinished organizations. Thus, please allow this to be a warning for all educators and a plea that their desire to remain unfinished also allows them to adjust and adapt as the curriculum does. It is okay for all of us in education to have some tolerance for ambiguity and some flexibility in the push and pull for innovative practices and standards aligned curriculum.

Standards

Standards, by and large, are created at the national level. Occasionally, this is the direct work of the United States Department of Education and other times standards are originated by large, reputable organizations representing teachers of a particular discipline. Different states have differing opinions on individual standards and sets of standards, but universal standards serve as the backbone of curriculum.

In district after district, school leaders promote their "standards aligned" curriculum. What is being taught and how it has been determined to be essential are the foundation of the very essence of serving as a teacher. Standards are a significant part of our work, but understanding how and why they have been developed will assist the unfinished teacher in their quest to conceptualize the greater context impacting the educational environment.

If we look at American educational history from 1983 to today, it is clear how we entered the era of accountability. First, was the publication of "A Nation at Risk" during the Reagan administration. That eventually fostered the data-based accountability system promoted through No Child Left Behind during the George W. Bush administration. The newest iteration was dubbed Race to the Top and issued during the Obama administration.

The intent of this section is not to politicize the educational environment. As such, we will not get into the think tanks, financial backing, and corporate influence over standards. Instead, anyone reading this is encouraged to remember all standards that have been created and implemented to help guide our practice.

A book by Cohen and Slover (2022), *Unfinished Agenda: The Future of Standards-Based School Reform* illustrates what is meant by "high-quality, standards aligned curriculum:"

> The curriculum should be rigorous and grade-level appropriate and provide students with the opportunity to build knowledge and skills and develop strong relationships with teachers and other students. It should include texts and topics that affirm students' identities and appeal to their interests; help them learn about, understand, and develop empathy and respect for others; and empower them to be agents of change in their own lives.

As an unfinished teacher, you'll be called upon to "align to the standards" and to know and understand the standards to which your curriculum is aligned. The job seems simple but is complex. Educators are not just charged with creating cohesion and alignment with the teachers delivering the same content, but also with teachers working with similar students both prior to and after them.

This is difficult, but relatively straightforward to understand. The more complex, long-standing challenge across the nation is figuring out which standards to teach. Most educational researchers agree that there is nowhere close to enough time to adequately teach every standard. So, teachers are often put in the precarious position of figuring out what to teach, what not to teach, and how long to spend on any given topic.

We debate the merits of a curriculum that is a mile wide or an inch deep. And it seems that new topics and curriculum are added to our schools on an annual basis. The unfinished teacher should use standards as a firm guide and foundation, but also understand that within those parameters there is room for their growth and their passion to shine through.

Unfinished is a mindset. It is one that is necessary to weather the perpetual storm of change that surrounds standards, curriculum, and instruction.

Assessment

We spend a lot of time on assessment in our educational system. If you were to add up the hours of learning time used on test prep, quizzes, tests, standardized exams, reviews, and the like, it would be staggering. Imagine if all that time could be spent on more learning and less assessing. Now forget that because it's not likely going to happen. Instead, let's focus on how any assessments given are truly meaningful for our students.

If an assessment merely results in a letter or number grade that is written on a page or keyed into a gradebook, we are missing the point. In the 1983 movie *A Christmas Story*, Ralphie famously receives a C+ on a paper in his classroom. There is no explanation, there is no writing conference, and there is no reflection and growth. In any way, will that assessment lead to improvement on his next writing piece? The answer is clearly No.

So, truly, assessment is an informative practice on a two-way street. It should help a student know what they know and where they can improve. What changes do I need to make as a student moving forward? The other side of the street is for the teacher. Did my students comprehend what I expected them to? What changes do I need to make as a teacher moving forward? Assessment should impact practice on both sides of that street, not merely notate a score or status.

Assessment primarily takes on two forms. There are fancier adjectives and descriptions, but at its simplest form assessment is either *for* learning or *of* learning. When assessment is *for* learning, it speaks to the mindset guiding this book which describes all of us as unfinished and developing.

Westman (2018) suggests that formative assessment ensures students are learning. Formative assessment is synonymous with assessment *for* learning. Formative assessments are ongoing, just-in-time assessments used by the teacher to check on the learning and teaching. She goes on to share some questions that help teachers determine what type of formative assessment to use, from page 64:

- What am I trying to assess (skill, standard, understanding of concept)?
- What type of assessment is most likely to assess this (multiple choice, performance assessment, written response)?
- Where does the student need to go next?
- How will I use the information from the formative assessment to adapt my next steps?

Abandon exit tickets. Yes, you read that correctly. Exit tickets *rarely* lead to a dramatic shift in instruction or immediate remediation. Use the exact same exit ticket but give it ten minutes earlier. The on-the-fly adjustments that brilliant teachers will make better serve the instructional needs of the students in the classroom. Trust us, give this one a try.

When we think of assessments *of* learning, we often speak about summative tests, standardized tests, end-of-chapter, or end-of-unit exams. If assessments *for* learning allow us to adapt on the fly for individual student needs, then assessments *of* learning allow us to adapt our programming and curriculum from unit to unit and year to year.

The real takeaway here is that assessment provides data that should always lead teachers to action. If you are unwilling to change your adult behaviors because of the data, it is not worth the time spent collecting it.

CHAPTER SUMMARY

As authors we recognize that not everything in the curriculum realm is in the direct control of teachers, and we (as practicing administrators) know that teacher agency and voice are imperative. Often, we have seen examples of teacher voice and agency being overlooked in systems. We hope a takeaway is that teacher voice and agency, plus administrator voice and agency, plus student voice and agency, plus community voice and agency is the right formula for productive change and lasting impact.

Philosophically, we are moved by what Maya Angelou once said: "Do the best you can until you know better. Then when you know better, do better." That's really the essence of the book and all the subject matter. We're unfinished, on a continual quest to become the next version of ourselves. We're never done. We are doing the best we can until we know better, then we do better. Whether we have direct or indirect control of the large or the small, let's do the absolute best we can every day.

Tomorrow Takeaways

- Spend some time with your organization's teaching and learning department administrators to get the clearest understanding of what your organization believes with respect to curriculum, standards, assessment, and data.
- Remember that we are a data-informed, people-driven profession. Data does not drive us; it informs us. People drive us!
- Assessment for learning can transform your impact as a teacher and helping each child learn in a planned, meaningful way can make a huge difference every day for every child.
- Join the curriculum committee and make sure your voice is heard. We can and must unite for the betterment of our schools.

Reflection Questions

- Is your data on the two-way street impacting both student self-knowledge and teacher professional practice?
- In what ways are you creating awesome, memorable moments for your students via the curriculum? What lessons will kids talk about years from now?
- Have you considered professional development opportunities where you can maximize or increase your knowledge and understanding of curriculum and assessment?
- How frequently do you engage in professional development conversations with fellow teachers?
- If you don't, can you think of ways to deliberately start to create "curriculum" conversations with one another?

6

Meeting the Needs of Each Child

"Equity can never become reality in schools if we look at it through the lens of Charity instead of professional obligation."

—Dr. Anthony Muhammad *(foreword of* Ruthless Equity*)*

Guiding Question: For this chapter, the guiding question comes from Ken Williams's book *Ruthless Equity*. How are you intentional about creating a culture of belonging in your classroom?

A Teacher Said to Us: "There are thirty of them and only one of me. Sometimes it feels like I cannot ever do enough or be enough for all of my students."

VOICES

As we begin this chapter, it is important to address two core issues. First, equity can be a scary term. In some communities the mention of equity will bring scrutiny and vilification brought about by the large political divides in the United States at the time of publication. Second, we want to acknowledge the potentially oblivious nature of the three older white gentlemen (using that term loosely) authoring this chapter.

The response to each of these issues is interrelated. First, equity is simply at the heart of education. The term has been hyper-politicized, but this section will help the unfinished teacher understand how to best navigate these issues in an apolitical manner (when possible) to still bring the best to their kids.

Secondly, we believe the conversation is worth having no matter who is leading it. While there is no contention that there may be voices better suited to discussing topics such as equity, we believe that the platform provided by this book demands that we bring this topic into focus. We, as three white men, seek out help, support, guidance, and clarity from friends, colleagues, and leaders of different backgrounds from us on a regular basis.

EQUITY

Equity is a huge buzzword lately; but equity has been at the core of education forever. At its core, equity simply means meeting the unique needs of each child every day. When depoliticized it is hard to imagine someone arguing that at our best, educators do whatever it takes to make the educational process meaningful and appropriate for each child. That is quite simply how we choose to view and define the pursuit of equity in education.

Equity and equality are often confused or used interchangeably. According to the dictionary, equity is the quality of being fair and impartial, and equality is the state of being equal, especially in status, rights, and opportunities. Equity is not necessarily the same treatment—but fair treatment. This is difficult to operationalize for standardized education professionals. That's why it's so important that we, as unfinished teachers, strive for equitable access to educational excellence vs equal access.

There is a meme/infographic that is commonly used to explain equity on social media. The setting is that of three children, one tall, one short, and one in the middle standing behind a fence. On the other side of the fence is a baseball game they would like to watch. Next to them are three boxes.

In the graphic depicting equality, all three children stand on one box. The issue is that the tall child did not need the box to see over the fence in the first place and the short child still cannot see over the fence despite standing on one box. The graphic depicting equity shows the tall student who could already see over the fence without a box, the middle student with one box and able to see over the fence, and the short child with two boxes and the ability to see the game.

This graphic explains equity at its basic level. Some, further, take the fence away and say that "liberation," as evidenced by the removal of the barriers in the first place, should be the goal. As an unfinished teacher, it will be impossible to remove every systemic barrier that may be in place. In our classrooms, however, much autonomy exists for each teacher to be a champion to be a champion for kids. Teachers have the autonomy to work hard to provide what they need to be successful.

Unfinished teachers are equity focused; they create conditions of welcome, rigor, positivity, and justice for each child under their care. That said, context matters. Every child needs a champion, but an acute understanding of the rules, regulations, expectations, and community norms is paramount. With these understandings, the unfinished teacher would be able to navigate the politics in the classroom and in the community.

It may seem easier to not engage in this type of dialogue or discussion at all. The answer is that it probably is easier, but most people did not go into education because it was easy. The best teachers went into education because they know that it matters. Doing what is best for each kid, every day, absolutely matters.

We do this because we know that we have a professional obligation to meet the needs of each child every day. It's exhausting and exhilarating at the same time. We don't "do" equity work, we "are" equity work. The responsibility for equity rests with each one of us.

COLLECTIVE EFFICACY

Collective efficacy in a school building is one of the most powerful strategies that can impact student performance. This is not just our opinion. This is one of the core findings of John Hattie's *Visible Learning*. The thing is, however, that collective efficacy is not really a strategy. Collective efficacy is largely a belief system.

Sarah Sugarman explains collective efficacy in the following manner:

> Collective efficacy occurs when teachers in a school believe that, as a team, they have the power to help their students learn more effectively—and this belief is based on their own shared experiences of success. A culture of collective efficacy does not simply happen; it is built intentionally.

Collective efficacy simply means that as a professional, the unfinished teacher believes in their ability to change outcomes for kids. When that belief exists, there is ownership and agency in the educational process. When that ownership and agency exists, education has no limits.

When we own the results that our students produce and understand our ability to impact their outcomes, we are compelled to help create educational conditions where each child, every day, has access to excellent educational opportunities. They get what they need to grow. This is our mission. This is equity.

Collective efficacy exists when a group of people have two core beliefs. First, that the future can be better than the present. Second, that they have influence and agency to make the future a better place. With those two core beliefs, every single teacher has what it takes to be a champion for collective efficacy, a champion for equity, and what it takes to always remain unfinished.

A core adversary to collective efficacy is known as BCD. BCD is an acronym that stands for "blame, complain, defend." This concept was popularized in Urban Meyer's book *Above the Line*. It denotes that whenever someone is avoiding ownership and/or working to preserve the status quo, a common psychological and verbal pattern emerges. This means that people commonly think and/or articulate these excuses or defense mechanisms.

What happens first when people do not want to take accountability or want to preserve the status quo is blaming someone or something else for their problem. The next step is to complain about their current situation or circumstances surrounding the problem or change in front of them. Lastly, the person defends their previous behavior as a justification for either not taking responsibility or avoiding change.

This phenomenon is pervasive far outside the world of education, but for the sake of the unfinished teacher, consider this very real educational example. Imagine a faculty meeting where an administrator is going to show data from a standardized assessment that did not go well for the students in the building.

In this scenario, can you imagine several colleagues saying things like: "This test does not mean anything because as seventh graders they know it does not count for anything and they don't care. Additionally, we know we have the shortest day and the least amount of math instructional time. You can say anything you want to about that data, but I will trust my local data and 83 percent of my kids are getting As and Bs."

While this is a theoretical example, it likely rang very true to many of the readers of this book after having sat through a meeting with very similar discourse. This is not intended to call out those teachers who make remarks such as that. It is instead a call to state that we cannot meet the needs of all children without an acute sense of ownership and responsibility. There is no way for us to foster this ownership and responsibility without true collective efficacy.

With collective efficacy, teachers do whatever it takes to create the outcomes for kids that they desire. With collective efficacy, we hold each other accountable, and we unearth and debunk those individual and systemic biases. Without collective efficacy, schools find excuses and convince themselves that their excuses are worthy of outweighing their ability to impact change on behalf of children.

TREATING EACH CHILD AS THEY NEED TO BE TREATED

Equity is frequently summarized by the mantra of "meeting the needs of each child." Hence the title of this chapter. Many, you guessed it, buzzwords and initiatives are derived from here. These range from individualized education, personalized education, differentiated education, and even to individualized education plans.

All these academic undertakings that for decades have been commonplace are sincere manifestations of a drive for equity. In the white paper from Education Reimagined, their North Star vision is to provide personalized, contextual, and relevant learning experiences for kids.

Most importantly, in our eyes, is that this writing stands firm with the presupposition that children desire to learn. The mindset shift from "we have to convince students to learn" to "they already want to learn" is a game changer. We just must make it relevant to them and their particular contexts. To adopt that mindset, the individual needs of each child must be considered when making instructional decisions.

As an example of this, recently an administrator we know was able to watch a veteran teacher instruct a lesson on *The Great Gatsby*. The lesson was different, quirky, and related the book to popular social media content that went right over our heads. The kids absolutely loved it, and the data from the formative assessment showed almost everyone hit the objective for the day.

After the lesson, when asked about the effectiveness of the lesson, the teacher opined that she scrapped the normal plan because she knew her high-school-age child would have hated it and went with something he would have engaged with. Context matters. Perspective matters. The unfinished teacher meets the students where they are and not just where the educator may want them to be.

RESPONSE TO INTERVENTION (RTI) / MULTITIERED SYSTEM OF SUPPORTS (MTSS)

One of the largest initiatives that has been present in American education to meet the needs of each child in recent years has been the RtI / MTSS movement. When explained, this process makes all the sense in the world and seems intuitive in nature. While there are many more and significantly complex books on RtI and MTSS, this is intended to instruct an unfinished teacher on how they should approach the process.

As teachers know and do very well, if the core curriculum and primary instruction does not yield data-based results, a second tier of intervention is necessary where (often) other professionals in the building work to help serve the students and better meet their needs (speech, psychologists, interventions, specialists, etc.). If this process still does not produce results, a more formalized and intensive protocol would be put in place to ensure each student is receiving exactly what they need.

The role of the unfinished teacher is largely in the first phase of this process. This is what takes place in the classroom. Johnson and Williams (2015) wrote in their book "premised on the idea that, to eliminate gaps in achievement and outcomes, students must have access to quality instruction every day" (99). Meeting the needs of each child every day is the aim of the unfinished teacher.

This is meant to be a review or affirmation for our teacher readers. What happens if the needs of each child every day are not met? Then our collective work as equity ninjas has fallen short. The challenges we surface in the book, and the challenges you know in your mind and daily observations that exist is that at times, the systems in which we work are limiting. We need to disrupt those limiting systems so that the collective "we" can and do meet the needs of each child every day.

The most important characteristic of successful curricular or intervention programs is that all teachers involved in the education of a student have ownership of that student's progress. In unsuccessful programs, nobody owns the data or takes responsibility. In successful programs, everybody takes ownership of the data and thereby the performance and needs of each individual student.

We assert that these ten foundational questions should be considered at the teacher and building levels to assess the implementation of an intervention program. Over time we each have seen that collaborative discussion answering each of these ten questions allows for clarity in process and the identification of gaps.

1. Does your program measure success by determining whether or not the process is creating more than typical growth?
   - Intervention should close gaps, not make adequate annual growth.
2. Does your program place the most needy kids with the least trained professionals?
   - Intervention programs often place the most at-risk students with noncertified employees and leave the other students making adequate progress with their teachers.
3. Does the scheduling of remediating student skill deficiency rank above, alongside, or below electives, social science, science, etc.?
   - Scheduling is an issue with intervention. There is no correct answer, but this question must be dealt with. Our scheduling is representative of our priorities.

4. Is there a scientific—or even a systematic—process as to what students receive what interventions?
   - Too often every student receives the same intervention regardless of the reason they landed in intervention. If a student's problem is with number sense and another student struggles with math facts, they need different support.
5. Are the interventions provided used to the extent necessary to allow for research-supported results?
   - Oftentimes interventions are not provided with the amount of time necessary to be implemented with fidelity.
6. Does anyone own the results the students are producing?
   - As mentioned above, in successful systems everyone owns the student progress and data. The data belongs to the student, the teacher, the administrator, the interventionist, and everyone involved.
7. Do teachers view it as their ultimate responsibility to provide differentiation within the classroom as the first stage of the RtI / MTSS process?
   - Step one is always inside the classroom as a means of finding how to deliver what each individual student needs.
8. Are interventions aligned to identified skill deficiencies or are they aligned to the calendarized curriculum?
   - Too frequently intervention programs become homework help instead of addressing the more pressing, underlying issues.
9. Is every classroom designed to attempt to maximize every minute of every day for every kid?
   - Many times students who are meeting standards are ignored, and school can become boring and less impactful for them.
10. Is the process in and out of intervention fluid or can a student get stuck in "intervention purgatory"?
    - Too often systems force kids into intervention for a predetermined set of a time with no escape if they have closed the initial gap which placed them in the program in the first place.

CHAPTER SUMMARY

As an unfinished teacher, we encourage you to provide access to whatever your students need for success. We assert that if you have an undying belief in your ability to impact the outcomes of your students that this will occur more naturally than not. Lastly, the most systematic approach to this at the building and district level is usually wrapped into a documented intervention protocol.

While some teachers forgive themselves of the responsibility of moving students forward once they are on the caseload of an interventionist, the unfinished teacher never quits owning their students' progress and making the necessary adjustments to meet them where they are at.

The key for equity for the unfinished teacher is working diligently to provide the best educational inputs and outputs so we can support learning and growth every day for every child. The great part is that this is easily observed in schools every single day. Teachers do remarkable work of scaffolding when it is necessary, reteaching when data indicates some children need it, and using technology to modify lessons to meet the needs of all learners.

Tomorrow Takeaways

- Abandon all BCD (Blame, Complain, Defend) behaviors to create more ownership of student progress.
- Conduct a personal or school-wide intervention assessment given the ten questions in this chapter.
- Equity does not need to be controversial. In fact, it is at the heart of everything we do in education.
- Each child deserves equitable access to educational opportunities. This can be done, and we need one another for the answers on how.

Reflection Questions

- What are some foundational beliefs you have about teaching and learning and education in general? (Sanfelippo and Zoul 37)
- In what ways do you review your core values? Do you list them? Refer to them? Is your classroom work reflective of those core values?
- In what ways are you consciously measuring student perceptions of inclusion or belonging in your classroom or school?
- Are you engaging in dialogue or reflective conversations about "equity"? If yes, with whom? If no, why not?
- Each child deserves equitable access to educational opportunities. In what ways are you making this a reality?

7

Technology

"Technology is not just a tool. It can give learners a voice that they may not have had before."

— George Couros

Guiding Question: The guiding question for this chapter comes from Lisa Westman's book *Student-Driven Differentiation*. How do you ensure that technology positively impacts differentiation?

A Teacher Said to Us: "I know technology is a bigger part of my students' world than it ever was of mine. I'm still trying to figure out how to embrace and incorporate that reality while minimizing the distractions that technology brings."

TECHNOLOGY AS AN ENABLER

There may be no better concept to explore remaining unfinished than that of technology. Technology really exemplifies and embodies the unfinished concept. The generation-to-generation growth of different iterations of technology is arguably the most dominant force impacting societal change. Technology is changing at a radical and exponential rate. Our challenge as educators is to try and change at a commensurate speed.

The unfinished teacher embraces the concept of technology as an enabler for augmenting and enhancing education, teaching, and learning. Technology is an ever-evolving tool that continues to redefine what education *can* look like. These consistent changes can be intimidating for a teacher who spends an inordinate amount of time learning one means of technology before promptly needing to learn another.

The bottom line is that technology serves as an enabler to students, teachers, and school systems allowing access to high-quality education and support to be democratized and available to all students.

As the CoSN (the Consortium for School Networking, cosn.org) has noted, the three top Tech Enablers for 2023 are Artificial Intelligence (AI), Untethered Broadband and Connectivity, and a Rich Digital Ecosystem. These enablers are not "maybe" things. These enablers must be embraced as we have no choice as educators but to produce citizens ready to thrive in a society flooded with technology. We simply cannot allow schools to be the least technologically advanced environment our students experience.

In addition to the enablers, the concept of being unfinished calls for the teacher to learn and apply how to use tech enablers to best amplify students' voices and, ultimately, students' learning. Artificial Intelligence (AI) is a bit terrifying right now; we think everyone can admit that. It is also amazing and bends our reality a little bit.

We must embrace this shift, remembering that many educators were also terrified of Google in 2000. Remember that however complex AI is right now, this is the least sophisticated version that will exist moving forward. It's only getting better and more complex every day.

Now, here is a sobering reminder for your forty-five- to fifty-five-year-old authors.

Many readers of this book who are in the early stages of their teaching careers were barely born in the year 2000. And they do not remember being terrified by Google or AI—it's the only world they know. Carried further, they were in grade school when iPads came out. The world, in our multigenerational educational institutions, holds a fascinating social construct difference for each of us with respect to technology as a concept.

The key is simple, *mindset*. If we embrace thinking like an app, we can be open to the idea that we, like technology, are constantly evolving as we learn, grow, "update," etc. When you open an app, you often can see what version you are opening. Sometimes it is version 12.4. This often just means it is the twelfth iteration of the product, and essentially the fourth draft of this iteration.

Our challenge to you is to consider whether you are updating yourself as frequently as your favorite app does. Can you commit to learning new things, deploying new strategies, and always evolving as often as your favorite game, social media app, or website? The thought of technology might make you cringe.

If you believe that technology has infiltrated and is ruining school, consider this for one minute. In a typical classroom, technology itself is ever present. It's in the heating control system, the lighting system, the TV or projection systems, the teacher's computer, the document camera, the student phones and tablets, and possibly in the classroom security system.

Technology is an enabler all around us. Technology has become ubiquitous. There are likely no career paths or futures for our students that do not involve the integration of technology.

LEVERAGE FOR GOOD—EMBRACE THE REALITY OF THE STUDENT WORLD

Imagine for a moment what technology means to a typical student today. They have a phone or a device or a tablet at pretty much all ages. They text or use apps to communicate with peers. There are too many to name and many of them come and go as frequently as we adults figure out what they are. Their world is a technology dominated world.

Can you even imagine a technology-free day? Neither can we. We've come to depend on spell-check, grammar check, translation tools, research/reference tools, automatic climate control, lighting, traffic control as we drive to work, even the various safety features on modern automobiles, which are all powered by technology.

A very real critique of technology is the fact it serves as a distractor in the classroom. There is truth to that. We have never met a teacher that is more fun than getting lost in a string of algorithmically designed social media reels for twenty minutes. One trick to becoming a master technology leader is to learn how the students interact with their world and environment. Then you can mirror and leverage that for application into your learning environment, often with tools enabled by and powered by technology.

Technology is absolutely providing access to our world for students whose exposure may have previously been bound by their geography, parents, and network television. It is amazing and almost impossible to think about how liberating technology tools are for so many of us every day. Technology literally opens the world to us. Writing this has been interesting, because we are so integrated with technology that we may not even realize its impact on our world.

GAMIFY/ARTIFICIAL INTELLIGENCE (AI)/AUGMENTED REALITY (AR)/MIXED REALITY (MR)

On September 27, 1998, the Baltimore Ravens defeated the Cincinnati Bengals 31–24. But that's not why that game is significant. During that professional football game, Sportvision Inc. premiered the yellow virtual first down line. This augmented reality tool has transformed the way the world watches American football.

Let's turn back the clock—the very first NFL game ever broadcast on TV was between the Brooklyn Dodgers and the Philadelphia Eagles on October 22, 1939. The fans that day could never have imagined a virtual first down line. So that begs a very important question. What technological realities lie ahead in sports broadcasting that current fans cannot possibly imagine.

More importantly, how does this same thinking play out in our classrooms and our educational systems? What will the next twenty years bring to our classrooms? What will the next two to three years bring? In what ways are we, as teachers, preparing students for a future we can't even imagine yet? The NFL and its fans never saw augmented reality coming to their sport either.

Students engage in video games and technology games, tasks, encounters, experiences, social interactions every day. They avail themselves of artificial intelligence (AI) in so many ways (grammar tools, Siri, Alexa, GPS, ChatGPT, navigation, and so much more). Often educators scoff at the idea of gamifying education, particularly as students exit the fifth grade. Why, because junior high and high school should be more like the real world? The reality is that we have a great glimpse into how the brain works and how to sustain a child's attention. And, the real world is *full* of technology.

This should be incredibly exciting for us, and whatever is working to keep a twelve-year-old's attention for eighty minutes is something that must be considered when we are designing instruction. Gamification of the classroom may not be the answer, but it, or components of it, should certainly be considered.

Whether our student is to become an automaker, a butcher, an Air Force pilot, or a teacher themselves, they engage in elements of gamification in real life and in our schools. What should be considered, and is an absolute imperative moving forward, is the fact that we must embrace and maximize the value of artificial intelligence and augmented reality tools in our classrooms. These are *not* going away. They are present in everything our students observe on a daily basis and will undoubtedly be present in their future endeavors as professionals.

The point in sharing that is that, for these tools to move our schools forward, they are dependent upon the amazing teacher to get that work done. Educators must unite to move learning forward on behalf of each child every day. Technology is unfinished just like we are. AI, gamification, and other technological trends will not fix all that ails us in education. They are tools, and they are part of the world we live in.

They are ever evolving and improving tools that as educators we can figure out how to leverage so that our students have the best possible experience in school and preparation for success outside of schools. We can do anything. Technology tools help us become the next versions of ourselves and create the next conditions of learning for our students.

SEEKING PROFESSIONAL DEVELOPMENT AND GROWTH

So much of "just-in-time learning" is available at our fingertips via some type of technology. Whether we're attending graduate school via our laptop and webcam or whether we're communicating with other educators on anything via a webinar format, we can learn anywhere and anytime. So can our students. No longer *should* geography dictate access to the highest quality education for our students. Period.

We can learn from just about anyone at any time. Major universities are putting free and low-cost content on the web so we can efficiently and effectively access learning all the time. These are commonly referred to as MOOCs (Massive Open Online Courses). This may sound amazing. At the time of this writing, MOOCs are already fifteen years old. This is a great example of how some educators who chose to stay unfinished have been exploring and leveraging this technology while others were unaware it even existed.

As we are all acutely aware, learning in a digital world is not always formal. Twitter (now called "X") has been a game changer for the three of us. Twitter (now called "X") chats are one of so many examples of free, online learning for all of us at any time. Not only have we connected with and become lifelong friends with others after communicating with them via Twitter (now called "X") chats, it has also dramatically impacted the trajectory of our careers. This topic was concisely explored in Mike and Nick's first book, *The Unlearning Leader*.

> An educational chat is like a one-hour conference call, meeting, or symposium. All that is needed is a Twitter (now called "X") account, an hour of time, and an open mind about digital professional learning. . . . Whether someone is already a Twitter (now called "X") user or not, they can search these hashtags to get a sense of how . . . Twitter (now called "X") use communicates and shows the districts' stories as well as the real-time learning experiences and opportunities for students, staff, and community. Similarly, the voice of educational leadership, digital leadership, and general leadership is amplified by [a variety of educational chats]. (Chapter 4)

You can use technology to expand your circle and your influence. Find your people and connect, collaborate, and create. We are proud to say that our relationship, although we are all Illinois educators, started through online learning together and choosing to stay connected.

STUDENT LENS/AGENCY

As the George Couros quote at the top of this chapter states, *"Technology is not just a tool. It can give learners a voice that they may not have had before."* The aims of technological tools and interventions can be and perhaps, should be, designed to give learners a voice, agency, and elements of personalized learning environments.

Schools are learning institutions. All humans in a school should be always learning. Student learning and growth and the conditions we create to support that learning and growth are the bread and butter of the teacher's work. Beyond that, the focus on the organization should be on the growth and learning of all people within the organization.

Well-functioning schools, ideally, are set up to support learning and growth for everyone, students, staff, community. Technology tools can be and should be used to support this growth and learning. In fact, the only way this can be done at scale is through leveraging technology to make this happen. It is not an *if*, it is how well, and what comes next.

TECHNOLOGY IS UBIQUITOUS

The unfinished teacher does not view nor use technology in place of teaching and support, they use technology as an enhancement where appropriate, to their conditions that support learning and growth. Technology itself is ubiquitous, it's everywhere. To be clear, the fact that students are good with technology and that it is already everywhere is a point of leverage for amplifying their seemingly natural gifts.

This is true for some students, but not all students. This is not to be used as an excuse for not becoming well-versed in technology yourself. Students may be able to lead on this, but they should be leading alongside an unfinished educator. Lisa Westman outlines five major ways this can be done. Her work focuses on how technology tools can be used to enhance the teacher/student/home relationship.

Westman's work was amplified because it is not just her experience that dictates her suggestion. She also cross-references John Hattie's paramount work and best-in-field research to determine effect sizes for interventions. Westman highlights the following in her writing about digital portfolios:

- Student Goal Setting (.5 effect size)
- Teacher Student Feedback (.75 effect size)
- Student Progress Toward Mastery (1.44 effect size)
- Examples of Mastery Learning (.58)
- School-Home Communication (.52)

Westman's work is so powerful because it shows that doing technology for technology's sake is not necessary. Notice that technology may be present, but it isn't the driving force. Integrated technology into the classroom is the best thing we can do for kids to create the best possible outcomes, but it needs to be married to solid pedagogy.

Even in 2023, we all know people who claim that they "don't do technology." To be clear, this is not an ageist statement. People from all generations are still resistant to technology, even in education. After reading this chapter, that hopefully sounds as ridiculous as driver's education teachers teaching horseback riding because they "don't do cars."

As educators, we don't get to decide the makeup of the world our kids live in, and more importantly, the world they will live in in the future. However, we can all agree that technology will be a huge part of the rest of their lives. *So, when a teacher claims to be averse to technology, they are knowingly putting their students' reality aside for their own comfort.* Read that again.

CHATGPT AND GENERATIVE ARTIFICIAL INTELLIGENCE

ChatGPT (and/or competitors that will emerge) will forever change education. Either we embrace this and start to go on offense on how to best use it, or we stay on defense and lose the opportunity for progress.

To explain, look at the sophistication of writing that comes from ChatGPT on January 3, 2023, "What Is a Teacher?"

> A teacher is a person who helps others to learn, typically by teaching in a school or other educational institution. Teachers may work in other settings, such as museums or community centers, or teach online or privately. They may teach a wide range of subjects, including language, literature, history, science, math, and the arts. The main goal of a teacher is to help students acquire the knowledge, skills, and values they need to succeed in life. Teachers may use various teaching methods, such as lectures, discussions, hands-on activities, and multimedia presentations. They may also evaluate student progress and provide feedback to help students improve their learning. (cosn.org)

If you think that was an impressive mini-essay created in about ten seconds, then this will blow your mind. As Illinoisans, we had the privilege of talking to and planning with the director of TEDxWindyCity. At their next event, they plan to have a (what they believe to be the first) TED Talk entirely constructed through AI be presented. These tools are game changers!

In the school setting, the most important work with technology is to maximize student support. Whether it's for the whole group, small group, cooperative group, individualized learning, curriculum, assessment, or instruction, technology enablers are present and can be harnessed each day.

Let's embrace this more than as a passing fad of some sort as we go beyond electronic worksheets to genuine advancement of learning and growth via the vast and quite accessible technological tools at our fingertips. Adaptive learning models and smart applications are all around us. These apps, as powerful and dynamic as they may be, will not fix education. The most important element determining a child's success in school is still the quality of the teacher. And that will never change.

CHAPTER SUMMARY

This chapter started by reflecting on how technology is an enabler for so much in our society. The unfinished teacher embraces this for application in the classroom as an efficiency tool kit. Considering the ubiquitousness of technology allows us to leverage it for the good through the embrace of the student worldview.

Students interact with one another via apps, tools, devices, and other methods that are perhaps different from many of the teachers they encounter.

All in all, we suggest that the unfinished teacher lives like an app, always seeking improvement and updates. We should always be looking at ways to improve the students' learning and growth, in this case, using technology and its vastness as part of the overall teacher tool kit. We are never finished; we are always becoming the next versions of ourselves. We've said many times that you need to think of yourself like an app that is constantly updating throughout your career and your life. It shouldn't be lost on any of us that the actual apps on our phones and devices need to be updated by people. Those people who will be updating the apps on your favorite device in the future may very well be the students in your classroom today!

Tomorrow Takeaways
- Technology tools are everywhere, technology itself is ubiquitous, you can embrace the realities of communication, for example, to mirror the students' world and the world our students will soon enter.

- Think like an app. Always develop a better version of yourself. Always develop the next version of yourself.
- Learn and grow anywhere and anytime with the power in your fingertips. Create those same conditions of limitless learning every day for each child you teach, and technology can help you do this.
- You can use technology tools to give every learner agency and voice every day. The sense of urgency is that you not only can do this, but you must do this.

Reflection Questions

- Reflect upon the guiding question of this chapter: How do you ensure that technology positively impacts differentiation?
- In what ways are you enabling student-focused learning with technology tools?
- Do you ask for student input or voice in how to apply technology to the classroom?
- How would you react to a colleague who fears new technologies or says that they don't "do" technology?
- How do you confront your own fears regarding using technology in the classroom? Who can you go to for help?

- Think like an app. Always develop a better version of yourself. Always develop the next version of yourself.
- Learn and grow anywhere and anytime with the power in your fingertips. Create those same conditions of limitless learning every day for each child you teach, and technology can help you do this.
- You can use technology tools to give every learner agency and voice every day. The sense of urgency is that you not only can do this, but you must do this.

Reflection Questions

- Reflect upon the guiding question of this chapter: How do you ensure that technology positively impacts differentiation?
- In what ways are you enabling student-focused learning with technology tools?
- Do you ask for student input or voice in how to apply technology to the classroom?
- How would you react to a colleague who fears new technologies or says that they don't "do" technology?
- How do you confront your own fears regarding using technology in the classroom? Who can you go to for help?

8

Teacher and Staff Morale

I think the teaching profession contributes more to the future of our society than any other single profession.

—John Wooden

Guiding Question: How do we instill a positive and productive morale internally, with one another, and for our students?

A Teacher Said to Us: "Staff morale is at the lowest it's ever been. But I feel like I say that every year."

IT IS ALL OF US

It is complicated to talk directly about teacher and staff morale as a teacher. It is complicated, because the overall morale of a school is something that requires work and diligent effort from every member of the school community (teachers, administrators, educational support personnel, etc.). We authors are district leaders, we have served as school administrators, and we have been teachers too.

We have traveled to schools with an abundance of resources where staff say morale has never been lower because of one controversial or problematic situation. Correspondingly, we have been in schools fighting every possible financial, societal, and community battle with sincere reasons to have concern, say they are working in their own personal Disneyland. And we have been to schools in between.

Every single person plays a role in ensuring that the best possible school environment exists for kids. This includes that, as educators, we have a responsibility to ensure that we are doing everything we can to ensure our own morale stays positive whenever possible so that we can best serve others.

IMPACTS ON MORALE

According to a 2022 Gallup survey on employee morale, the six greatest threats (and conversely opportunities) to teacher morale include:

1. Personal safety and belonging
2. Time and resources
3. Leadership trust and values alignment
4. Ownership and input
5. Recognition and value
6. Professional growth

Given these six areas provided above, it is understandable as to why people in the educational field can feel undervalued and under an immense amount of pressure. The common structures of school pull against the very fabric of what research tells us builds morale.

Teachers are inundated with intimidating and scary safety drills, every minute of every day seems to be bound by expectations and direction, the most difficult and complex decisions are usually made with little impact, and recognition and growth opportunities are seemingly never in abundance.

The truth of the matter is that the job of education is equal parts beautiful and painful. For every unimaginable success story there is an unthinkable tragedy. In the words of our friend, Todd Whitaker—the great part about teaching is that it matters, the hard part is that it matters every day.

The ability to tackle this type of responsibility is not for the faint of heart because while the task is daunting, the opportunity to be the person to change the trajectory of a child's life is what makes this the best job in the world.

Every teacher deserves to work in an outstanding work environment that recognizes the hard work being put forth, gives them the resources to do so successfully, and provides them opportunities for growth. The ability of an individual teacher to control this is limited, but the one thing all educators can do is to remain focused on their individual journey and growth and how they best contribute to the overall morale of the school or district.

DIMENSIONS OF CULTURE

In many school districts around the country, they measure culture annually or multiple times per year. They work with consultants, organizational psychologists, professional associations, and other experts in the field of morale and culture/climate. They administer surveys then they share the results with all in the organization.

The key differentiator is that the successful implementation organizations then plan actions around the data. We have observed and studied successful organizations around culture, morale, and climate who make deliberate efforts and actions to share what was learned and to set goals collaboratively around what was learned to commit to actions that will lead to improvement. Replicate and continue what works. Terminate what is not working. Improve what is starting to work but has not yet taken hold.

In one of the many organizational culture surveys in use, one from consulting firm Humanex Ventures out of Kalamazoo, MI, measures organizational staff culture via the following dimensions of culture: Engage/Inspire, Continuous Improvement, Quality, Pride, Innovation, Satisfaction, Performance Planning, Talent/Fit, Relationships, Communication, Recognition, Career Development, Support-Equip, and Mission Conscious.

The instrument that measures culture asks the staff to rate/judge/evaluate/opine on their individual impact, the team impact, their supervisor's impact, and the overall organizational impact. How can you do this as a teacher in the classroom and in the building? Ideally, the environment is one where teachers have a shared stake in the leadership and in the organization of the school.

HEARING THE TEACHER'S VOICE

As a teacher, in what ways do you feel like you matter, like you belong, and like you have voice and agency? In what ways can the unfinished teacher step forward and join the committees, become the great teammate (we wrote about this in chapter 1), and support the belonging concepts for everyone? These are questions that will help increase the belonging feelings for our colleagues and ourselves and help build culture and morale.

It is most certainly the job of your administrators to make you feel recognized and valued. However, we are all responsible for creating the culture within our schools. When you think about the totality of all the people working in a school, it can be impossible to make everyone always feel that way. However, if we all commit to that lift—we can move the needle on culture.

Dr. Joe Sanfelippo is a superintendent, author, and speaker. In his book, *Lead From Where You Are*, he suggests a simple model for enhancing recognition and building culture—Recognize, Acknowledge, and Extend. It starts with all of us keeping our eyes and ears open to recognize the great things being done by our colleagues. When we see and hear those things, we need to take the time to acknowledge them.

It might be a conversation, a note, an email, or any other way to make that other person feel seen. Then comes the magic. Take that information and find ways to extend it. Tell another teacher what you saw. Give a shout-out at a meeting. Tweet about it. Put it in a newsletter. Ask them to present what they are doing at a conference. Extend it.

Creating a culture of recognizing, acknowledging, and extending can be a force multiplier when it comes to school culture. When these accolades come from the administration, they can often be viewed as "playing favorites" which can have a negative impact on culture and climate.

From peer to peer, it breaks down competitiveness and shows that we appreciate and value one another. Doesn't that sound like a great place to work every day? Joe says that culture is built thirty seconds at a time. Do you have thirty seconds today to make a colleague feel seen and recognized? Who is already doing this for you?

PARTNERING IN THIS WORK

Time and resources to do our jobs are critical elements in morale and culture and climate indices. As a teacher, do you have the time needed to prepare for your lessons, implement your instructional goals, assess student learning, and attend to the professional requirements of your role? If yes, you are likely to have higher and more positive morale. If not, you will see cracks in the armor of our schools and our feelings. Over time, morale and elements make and break the overall effectiveness of the school.

As an unfinished teacher, it's part of your DNA to continue to contribute to improving your use of time and your improvement of resources used to do all our jobs. Together with the administration and the leadership in the school and district, ideally, we're all working together to review the time we have and how we use it as well as the resources we have and their impact on our work and the student learning.

Meaningful professional growth and development opportunities go a long way toward improving morale. Teachers enjoy learning and growing. That's why we all went into this profession in the first place. When the organization can hear the voice of the teacher and put forth professional growth, that is a collaborative effort between teachers and administrators, the outcomes are better for the professionals and for the students, and it shows in the morale.

What is great to see, and we have seen this across the nation in various schools, when everyone takes the time to measure and report on the measures of morale (or culture or climate) then we are more likely see truly unique and positive outcomes for all. Peter Drucker is credited with saying that "culture eats strategy for breakfast" and that rings true across our industry.

Something outside of the control of the unfinished teacher is the trustworthiness of the administration. Nearly all administrators want positive morale to exist in the buildings. The teacher will thrive and benefit from an environment where the leadership is aligned with the teacher's core values and ethics. Alignment breeds success.

When the leadership is not trustworthy, the teacher faces a dilemma, and the overall morale will drop. It's at that crossroad where the teacher must decide if they can impact morale anyway or if they must weather the storm, or if they must make a different decision. Morale is a powerful force.

Recognition often ranks low in organizations, including schools. Some folks like private recognition, while others like public recognition. Teachers especially deserve acknowledgement and recognition as the work that is done is highly emotional and often draining. A little recognition goes a long way. If you aren't getting the satisfaction of receiving recognition, consider creating that feeling for others. Start a chain reaction that may very well find its way back to you in the future.

As a teacher, in what ways does the administration make us feel like we matter, like we belong, and like we have voice and agency? In what ways can the unfinished teacher step forward and join the committees, become a great teammate, and support the belonging concepts for everyone? These are questions that will help increase the belonging feelings for our colleagues and ourselves.

CHAPTER SUMMARY

How we feel at work will determine, in many instances, how we perform at work. It's imperative that we understand what impacts morale and how it impacts us as individuals. The unfinished teacher is a central cog in the wheel of the organization. The unfinished teacher is never satisfied with the status quo. They are always seeking to become the next version of themselves.

As we wrote, morale is "all hands on deck." It's everyone's business to focus on how we feel. It's up to us all to encourage and support one another. Especially in this current era of a critical shortage of teachers and administrators, it's essential we support one another to avoid burning out. Knowing the factors that lead to burn out can help us keep the candle lit and keep us mentally and physically healthy for ourselves, our students, and our organizations.

Dimensions of culture can be measured, analyzed, acted on and improved. It takes courageous and honest leadership from the top to the middle to all around to create conditions leading to positive and productive morale. If we do this work correctly, Drucker's famous quote could be amended to, "culture eats strategy for breakfast, lunch and dinner!"

Tomorrow Takeaways

- If your organization has not measured culture, climate, and morale, encourage the leadership to do so immediately to start the conversations.
- Consider measuring the morale of your classroom and your caseload to see how the environment is perceived by your students.
- Each one of us plays a role in the overall success of the organization. Make a plan, stick to it, and be part of the solution.
- Morale will always be a topic of conversation in schools. It's something we can all complain about, or it's something we can all work together on.

Reflection Questions

- Contemplate what Drucker's quote "Culture eats strategy for breakfast" means to you. How does this resonate with you and relate to your work and impact?
- What good things are happening in the building that you can Recognize, Acknowledge, and Extend?
- In your organization, in what ways is the morale conversation taking place? Is it formally measured as we have described? Is it informally measured with side conversations? How can you improve the morale in your organization?
- In what ways do the dimensions of culture as shared in this chapter resonate with you as a professional and as a practitioner with students?

Teacher Essay 2

My Unfinished Journey
Eric McFadden, High School Teacher

I remember when I first thought about becoming a teacher while I was in high school. I aspired to one day teach social studies and coach basketball. At the age of seventeen this seemed like a dream job. I loved learning and I couldn't get enough of basketball.

Of course, when you're a high school kid there are still a lot of things you don't know, and you look to the adults in your life for guidance. A friend of mine's dad was a teacher at our high school and when he learned of me wanting to teach, he vehemently discouraged it. He gave me the same story told until this day— "the money is no good, education is changing." So how I got here is a story of obstacles, detours, and opportunities.

After my conversation with my friend's dad, I started thinking about what else I was interested in doing. I really wasn't sure what I wanted to do. Those kinds of life decisions can be challenging for a teenager. I mean how was I supposed to know? I was a middle-class kid from a blue-collar family in the near south suburbs of Chicago.

I hadn't really been anywhere or experienced anything that shone a light on my future. I knew I was SUPPOSED to go to college. That was never really a question. What I was supposed to do when I got there was more of a mystery. So, in August 1992 I headed off to Bradley University with no declared major and no clear idea of what I wanted to do yet.

Bradley checked off a lot of boxes when I was looking at schools—mid-size, close to home, but not *too* close to home, a compact walkable campus, a computer in your dorm room (a big deal in 1992) and a program called the Academic Exploration Program.

The Academic Exploration Program was designed to give students with undeclared majors the opportunity to take classes within different colleges before deciding upon a major. Before long I knew what I wanted to do . . . well, sort of. I decided that I wanted to go into advertising.

I was always quite fascinated by the whole idea that advertising could influence the buying habits of people on such a mass scale. So, I declared my major in advertising with a marketing concentration. Little did I know that advertising jobs at the time were difficult to get, and the entry-level pay was abysmal.

College went fast and soon I was a senior and I wasn't really sure what I was going to do with the degree I was about to complete. I had taken a professional sales class in the College of Business, and learned that there were lots of companies that hired sales people out of college.

Okay, I certainly did not see myself as a professional salesperson when I left for college, but I was about to earn this degree and needed to do something. And so I began interviewing for sales positions. By spring break, I accepted a position at Canon where I would be selling copiers, fax machines, and printers.

As a twenty-two year old, working at Canon was pretty exciting. It felt very cool to put on a suit every day and meet new people. The sales staff was made up of a lot of people around my age, so the job also provided a lot of social opportunities and office camaraderie. Within two years, I was managing a team of seven salespeople and earning a pretty good financial living.

Unfortunately, the office equipment industry was also notorious for its high turnover due to the dog-eat-dog mentality. I decided that I had learned a lot from working at Canon, but it was time to move on. After all, it was the age of the dot-com, and the world was filled with new and exciting opportunities.

I left Canon to go work for an email marketing start-up. I would be working from home and starting to develop the business in the Chicago market. This sounded great. And the stock options sounded great . . . until they didn't. After a few months of working for the start-up, I was let go. It took a few months, but I found another sales job. But unemployment gave me a lot of time to self-reflect.

I took the job because I really needed to work, but I was starting to realize I did not want to be in sales for my entire life. My inner voice was calling out to me. It was that voice that led me back to grad school to do what I really wanted to do—teach! It took a couple more years in sales before I finally gathered the courage to pivot and go back to grad school to earn my teaching certificate.

While I was in grad school, I was fortunate to secure a substitute teaching job at the district that would eventually hire me for my current full-time position. At the time, teaching jobs, especially in social studies, were very competitive. I remember thinking to myself, how am I ever going to land a job?

Going to teacher career fairs at the time felt like an exercise in futility. I was literally standing in lines that could easily be an hour long just to hand my résumé to a school district and hope to make an impression in the one minute I might have to speak.

Fortunately, I started to build good relationships in the district where I was subbing. When interview season came around, I was given an interview. Even though I had gotten a foot in the door, I was nervous—there were hundreds of candidates who had applied for the three social studies positions available in the district.

After two rounds of intense panel interviews, I received a message while I was subbing asking if I could drive over to the other campus after school to meet in the district office. As I entered the conference room, I was extremely anxious. There were multiple district administrators in the room along with a couple of department chairs.

As I uneasily settled into a chair and greeted everyone, I had no idea what to think. Then the assistant superintendent spoke, "We have some good news and some bad news." He then explained that while the district was not going to hire me for a social studies position, they wanted to offer me a job in the business education department.

I wanted to scream for joy! While it wasn't exactly what I was planning for, I had landed a teaching job! I was so fortunate that while I was in grad school and had my college transcripts evaluated, I had taken enough business and computer courses in college to be certified in business education.

Teaching business was not at the front of my mind when I went back to grad school, but ultimately it worked out great. I was excited about the opportunity to work in the department, and I had gotten to know some of the people in the department during a long term sub assignment.

I began my teaching career teaching keyboarding, consumer education, and business computers classes, but one of the things you quickly learn when teaching in a mostly elective department is that you need to be able to evolve and be willing to teach new things. One morning in a weekly department meeting, our department chair announced she wanted to offer a video game design course and asked if anyone would be willing to learn how to do it and then teach the class.

Without any hesitation I volunteered. I was not much of a gamer, and I had no programming experience, but I knew this would be great for kids. Shortly after agreeing to teach this new class, I was selecting software and reading books to prepare. I really had no idea what I was going to be doing but I was determined to figure it out.

The first year teaching the class certainly had its challenges, and it was full of trial and error. Sometimes it would literally take hours to figure out how something was supposed to work correctly, which at times slowed down the pace of the class, but our kids were always super gracious much of the time we were learning together. As I continued to learn, the class got better and better. I finally got the class to the point where I could help kids troubleshoot problems much faster and teach them how to do more complex operations. Now it is one of my favorite classes to teach!

Three years ago, during remote learning due to the pandemic, my department chair asked if I might be interested in attending a virtual esports conference. I didn't have high hopes for a "virtual" conference, and I didn't know a lot about esports but I was intrigued. After attending the conference, I knew immediately that this was something our district needed to be doing.

I went back to my department chair to share with him what a great opportunity it would be to bring esports to our school. Afterward I set up a meeting with the superintendent, who was fully supportive of the idea. Having some extra free time during COVID-19 gave me the chance to draft a plan to implement an esports program with the goal of beginning the program the following fall when school would hopefully be open for in-person learning again. I spent some time promoting it to kids and holding virtual meetings to figure out what this new program would look like.

When the doors opened to school in the fall of 2021, we were ready to launch our esports program. I will never forget the first meeting when we had over one hundred kids show up! We would be competing in six different game titles as a part of the Illinois High School Esports Association. We were overwhelmed and excited about the number of kids who showed interest.

Our first season was a *huge* learning curve. There was so much to figure out. In our first day of tryouts, we discovered our computers were drawing too much power and we kept tripping circuit breakers. We had software updates that couldn't get past our network security and kids who didn't know how to log on to PCs.

Additionally, my assistant and I were holding tryouts for games that we ourselves didn't play! To say it was an adventure would be an understatement, but we came up with systems for tryouts, leaned on the IHSEA (Illinois High School Esports Association) for help, and worked closely with our tech team and building maintenance teams to make it all work.

As we began to settle in, our kids were having an absolute blast. Watching the players' teamwork, communication skills, and hand-eye coordination was amazing. And best of all is the gaming community is very inclusive and allows us to serve many students who would otherwise not be involved in a school activity.

And all our hard work and effort paid off in our inaugural year—we won the *Fortnite* state championship! What a great feeling for our players and program. A state championship! Then in year two of our program, we won another state championship in another game title. We were the *Rocket League* state champs! We are now serving over ninety students who play competitively and even more who come to play games recreationally.

If someone had told me twenty years ago that I would be teaching video game design and coaching an esports team, I would have laughed . . . and probably asked what esports were? As I tell my students all the time, life is not a linear path. We don't always know what roads we are going to end up following, but it's important to approach opportunities with an open mind and be a lifelong learner.

I don't know what adventures, challenges, and changes lie ahead. But my experiences have taught me to be open to whatever life brings.

9

Conclusion

Ambiguity. It's a scary word. If you are going to buy in to this idea of being an unfinished teacher, you must accept the ambiguity that comes with it. If you've made it to this point in the book, you've read vignettes from three teachers, one in the foreword, and two at the end of each section. A common thread from all three of those teachers was that twists and turns came during their careers and they had to be willing to accept change and develop into the next versions of themselves.

When we were younger, there were popular books called *Choose Your Own Adventure*. As you read through the book, you would be presented with options. When confronted with a dragon, turn to page x if you want to run away. Turn to page y if you want to fight the dragon. Turn to page z if you attempt to make friends with the dragon. This allowed you to have a unique reading experience as you made your way through the book. It was not just a story, it was now your story. Some parts of the book were out of your control, but others were very much in your control.

As an unfinished teacher, you get to choose your own adventure. Obviously, some aspects of your life and career are out of your control, but others are very much decisions that you get to make. When confronted with *that* dragon, which page will you turn to?

PAGE X—COMMIT TO A LONG CAREER AS A CLASSROOM TEACHER

There is no better and more meaningful career than being a teacher. We are the career that creates all other careers. Without teachers, there would be no doctors. Without teachers, there would be no lawyers. In fact, without teachers, there would be no teachers! We've heard people say that they are "just" a teacher. Knock it off! Teaching is an amazing calling and a fantastic way to spend your working years.

If you think that teaching will get easier the longer you do it, hopefully we have convinced you otherwise. If you are truly embracing the idea of being an unfinished teacher, you know that you must constantly evolve to meet the changes in our profession, and more importantly, the changing needs of our students.

You need to build strategies to take care of your physical, mental, and financial health. You need to be an active participant in writing curriculum and assessments in ways that are impactful for students. You need to seek ways to stay abreast of technology, value professional development, and own your role in building and sustaining the culture in your building. There is a growing teacher shortage in our country, so we need you more than ever.

PAGE Y—CONSIDER THE POSSIBILITY OF ADMINISTRATIVE ROLES

There is also a growing administrator shortage in our country. If you decide to go down this path, we suggest that you study the administrators you have worked with over the years. What qualities would you want to emulate in some leaders, and conversely, what qualities would you want to avoid as a future administrator?

If this is a path you choose, plan your graduate coursework to allow for the correct certifications and licensure. Seek opportunities to shadow school leaders and get involved with the things happening in your building. Maybe you can volunteer to help with the logistics of state testing or help organize a back-to-school event. Gather as many experiences and as much knowledge as you can along the way.

When we work with aspiring administrators, one piece of advice we give is that the very best way to get the future job you want is to be amazing at the job you currently have. No answer to an interview question will ever be more powerful than your work history, the relationships you have built, and the reputation you have forged over the years. Not everyone who wants to be an administrator always receives those jobs. And that's okay too. If the consolation prize is that you get to keep being an amazing teacher. There are countless kids in the future who will benefit from that outcome.

PAGE Z—LOOK AT OTHER OPTIONS OUTSIDE EDUCATION

It might seem strange for us to put this forward as an option as you choose your adventure. If you are not enjoying this profession, if you aren't feeling it, the most important decision you might make is to try something different. Not everyone is meant to be a teacher, and not every teacher is meant to be a teacher forever.

Life might take you home to care for children or parents. Life might take you back to school to change professions. Early on in this book, we talked about awareness. If you aren't happy and fulfilled in this role, it's okay to try something else. Your pathway may ultimately lead back to the classroom, it might lead to teaching in other places and other ways, or it might lead to more happiness and fulfillment in a different kind of role.

CLOSING WORDS

How do you finish a book about being unfinished? We hope we've made you think. . . . We hope we've provided some encouragement. . . . We hope you've learned a few things. . . . And most of all, we hope you'll join us on this journey, and stay . . .
Unfinished.

References

Achor, S. (2010). *The Happiness Advantage: The Seven Principles of Positive Psychology That Fuel Success and Performance at Work*. Cambridge, MA: Harvard University Press.

American Psychological Association. (2022). "Stress in America Survey." Retrieved from https://www.apa.org/news/press/releases/stress/2022/october-2022-topline-data.pdf.

Berkers, E., n.d. Enneagram Tests (free). [online] Eclectic Energies. Available at: https://www.eclecticenergies.com/enneagram/dotest.php.

Caposey, P. J. (2023). "Let's Move From Admiring Problems to Creating Solutions." Retrieved from https://www.ascd.org/blogs/lets-move-from-admiring-problems-to-creating-solutions.

Casas, J. (2020). *Live Your Excellence*. San Diego, CA: Dave Burgess Consulting, Inc.

Cheatham, J. P., Thomas, R., and Parrott-Sheffer, A. (2022). *Entry Planning for Equity-Focused Leaders: Empowering Schools and Communities*. Cambridge, MA: Harvard University Press.

Chenoweth, K. (2021). *Districts that Succeed: Breaking the Correlation between Race, Poverty, and Achievement*. Cambridge, MA: Harvard University Press.

Clear, James. (2018). *Atomic Habits: An Easy & Proven Way to Build Good Habits & Break Bad Ones*. New York: Penguin.

Cohen, M., and Slover, L. (2022). *Unfinished Agenda: The Future of Standards-Based School Reform*: Future Ed: Georgetown University.

Consortium for School Networking. "Discover the Top Hurdles, Accelerators, and Tech Enablers Driving K–12 Innovation in 2023. https://www.cosn.org/edtech-topics/driving-k-12-innovation/.

Covey, S. L. 1989. *The Seven Habits of Highly Successful People*. New York: Free Press.

EAB Teacher Morale Collaborative. "5 Reasons to Join the Movement to Raise Teacher Morale." https://eab.com/insights/expert-insight/district-leadership/5-reasons-raise-teacher-morale/.

Education Reimagined. "A Transformational Vision for Education in the United States." www.education-reimagined.org.

Equable. "Teacher Pensions in 2022." Retrieved from https://equable.org/teacher-pensions-in-2022/.

Fenwick, L. (2022). *Jim Crow's Pink Slip: The Untold Story of Black Principal and Teacher Leadership.* Cambridge, MA: Harvard University Press.

Fitzgerald, F. S. (2019). *The Great Gatsby.* Wordsworth Editions.

Fuchs, D., and Fuchs, L. S. (2006). "Introduction to Response to Intervention: What, why, and how valid is it?" Retrieved from https://www.uv.uio.no/forskning/om/helga-eng-forelesning/introduction-to-responsivenes-to-intervention.pdf.

Gallup's Q12 Employee Engagement Survey. Retrieved from https://www.gallup.com/q12/.

Hanson, Melanie. "U.S. Public Education Spending Statistics." Retrieved from EducationData.org, June 15, 2022, https://educationdata.org/public-education-spending-statistics.

Hattie, John. 2008. *Visible Learning.* London: Routledge.

Healy, T. J., Hess, C., and Nicholson, K. (2012). "Underfunded Public Pensions in the United States: The Size of the Problem, the Obstacles to Reform and the Path Forward." https://www.hks.harvard.edu/sites/default/files/centers/mrcbg/files/MRCBG_FWP_2012_08-Healey_Underfunded.pdf.

HumanexVentures. "INSIGHTeX." https://www.humanexventures.com/.

Johnson K., and Williams, L. (2015). *When Treating All the Kids the Same is the Real Problem.* Thousand Oaks, CA: Corwin.

Kurtz, H. (2022). "A Profession in Crisis: Results of the First Annual Merrimack College Teacher Survey." *Education Week.* Retrieved from https://www.edweek.org/research-center/reports/teaching-profession-in-crisis-national-teacher-survey.

Lubelfeld, M., Polyak N., and Caposey, P. J. (2018). *Student Voice: From Invisible to Invaluable.* Lanham, MD: Rowman & Littlefield.

Lubelfeld, M., Polyak N., and Caposey, P. J. (2021). *The Unfinished Leader: A School Leadership Framework for Growth and Development.* Lanham, MD: Rowman & Littlefield.

Lubelfeld, M., Polyak N. (2017). *The Unlearning Leader: Leading for Tomorrow's Schools Today.* Lanham, MD: Rowman & Littlefield.

Meyer, U. (2015) *Above the Line: Lessons in Leadership and Life from a Championship Season.* New York: Penguin Press.

Myers, I. B. (1962). "The Myers-Briggs Type Indicator: Manual (1962)." *Consulting Psychologists Press.* https://doi.org/10.1037/14404-000.

Pink, D. (2009). *Drive: The Surprising Truth About What Motivates Us.* New York: Riverhead Books.

Sanfelippo, J. (2022). *Lead From Where You Are: Building Intention, Connection, and Direction in Our Schools.* San Diego: IM Press.

Sanfelippo, J., and Zoul., J. (2022). *Crafting the Culture: 45 Reflections on what Matters Most.* Hanover, PA: ConnectedEDD Publishing.

Schneider, J., and Berkshire, J. (2020). *A Wolf at the Schoolhouse Door*. New York: The New Press.

Sugarman, S. (2021). "Three Actions for Building a Culture of Collective Efficacy." Retrieved from https://www.ascd.org/blogs/three-actions-for-building-a-culture-of-collective-ef-cacy.

Tyler, R. W. (1949). *Basic Principles of Curriculum and Instruction*. Chicago: University of Chicago Press.

Vander Ark, T., and Liebtag E. (2015). *Difference Making at the Heart of Learning*. Thousand Oaks, CA: Corwin.

Walker, Tim. (2022). "Beyond Burnout: What Must Be Done to Tackle the Educator Shortage." *National Education Association*. Retrieved from https://www.nea.org/advocating-for-change/new-from-nea/beyond-burnout-what-must-be-done-tackle-educator-shortage.

Westman, L. (2018). *Student-Driven Differentiation: 8 Steps to Harmonize Learning in the Classroom*. Thousand Oaks, CA: Corwin Press.

Williams, K. (2022). *Ruthless Equity: Disrupt the Status Quo and Ensure Learning for ALL Students*. Atlanta: Wish in One Hand Press.

About the Authors

Michael Lubelfeld, EdD, currently serves as the superintendent of schools in the North Shore School District 112 in Highland Park, Illinois, a north suburb of Chicago. Mike earned his Doctor of Education in curriculum and instruction from Loyola University of Chicago. He is also on the adjunct faculty at National Louis University and Loyola University Chicago in the department of educational leadership. Mike has earned an IASA School of Advanced Leadership Fellowship and he has also graduated from the AASA National Superintendent Certification Program. He can be found on Twitter (now called "X") at @mikelubelfeld and he is the co-moderator of #suptchat—the superintendent educational chat on Twitter. He and Nick Polyak authored the 2017 Rowman & Littlefield book *The Unlearning Leader: Leading for Tomorrow's Schools Today*. He, Nick, and PJ authored the 2018 Rowman & Littlefield book *Student Voice: From Invisible to Invaluable*, and the 2021 Rowman & Littlefield book *The Unfinished Leader: A School Leadership Framework for Growth and Development*. Mike was awarded the 2021 Administration and Supervision Distinguished Alumni Award from the Loyola University of Chicago School of Education. He and his wife Stephanie have two children, and they live in suburban Chicago.

Nick Polyak, EdD, is the proud superintendent of the award-winning Leyden Community High School District 212. He earned his undergraduate degree from Augustana College in Rock Island, IL, his master's from Governors State University, and his EdD from Loyola University Chicago. Nick has been a classroom teacher and coach, a building and district-level administrator, a school board member, and a superintendent for the past fifteen years in both central Illinois and suburban Chicago. Nick has earned an IASA School of Advanced Leadership Fellowship, was named a Superintendent of Distinction, and graduated from the AASA National Superintendent Certification Program. Nick directs the Transformational Leadership Consortium for the AASA. He can be found on Twitter (now called "X") at @npolyak and he is the co-moderator of #suptchat—the superintendent educational chat on Twitter. Nick and his wife Kate have four children and they live in suburban Chicago.

PJ Caposey, EdD, is an award-winning educator leading his small rural school to multiple national recognitions as a principal and has done the same as a Superintendent. PJ is an active member of the greater educational community voicing opinions and providing training and consultation on many topics. PJ is the author of more than ten books and is a sought-after speaker and consultant specializing in school culture, principal coaching, effective evaluation practices, and student-centered instruction. Recently, PJ has been named an NSPRA Superintendent to Watch, 40 Leaders Under 40 honoree, and Eastern Illinois University's Distinguished Educator Award winner. PJ currently serves as the Superintendent of Schools for Meridian CUSD 223 in Northwest Illinois and is married to his wife Jacquie and has four children. PJ is the 2022 Illinois Superintendent of the Year and a 2023 finalist for the AASA National Superintendent of the Year. PJ can be reached via Twitter (now called "X") @MCUSDSupe.

www.ingramcontent.com/pod-product-compliance
Lightning Source LLC
Chambersburg PA
CBHW030657230426
43665CB00011B/1138